ESCAPE!

I eased the door shut behind me and started down the aisle, pulling my jacket over the butt of the gun.

The exit door was twenty feet away—agonizingly distant. My back, turned toward danger, began to ache with anticipation of the blow I was sure would come. As I walked, a new fear seized me: that I would be seen by one of the hundreds of other enemy soldiers crowding this train.

When I reached the open door of the car, I looked back. There was no disturbance. I stepped back to the bottom mounting step. . . .

FOR GOD, COUNTRY, AND THE HELL OF IT

John Hickman

BALLANTINE BOOKS • NEW YORK

Library of Congress Catalog Card Number: 84-91157

ISBN 0-345-31853-6

Manufactured in the United States of America

First Edition: February 1985

To
my sons Lance and Steve
and to
the memory of their mother

PROLOGUE

This is the story of my personal encounter with the mighty German army in 1944, during World War II. On May 3 of that year my Mustang was so badly shot up by flak that I had to bail out over German-occupied northern France. I was taken prisoner, escaped, and with help from the French underground made my way to Switzerland. After three months in Switzerland, during which time the Allied forces landed in France, an English pilot and I slipped back into France and thumbed our way by air to England by way of Italy and North Africa, via Casablanca. I rejoined my squadron, operating out of a beat-up airfield near Paris, a little over four months after I'd been shot down.

I finished writing this tale in 1952 for my then infant sons, and their children following, as a record of what their ancestor did in the course of that historic encounter we call World War II. I thought I'd better set it down while the events were still clear in my mind, and before papers and records were scattered and lost, even though it would be some time before the youngsters would be able to read it.

Over the years since then I have read quite a few stories of wartime escape, most of them by Englishmen about Englishmen. Reading them has always left me disquieted, because the characters were all steely calm, ingenious beyond belief, and eight feet tall. The Germans were smart and tough, but it didn't take a superman to outfox them. After all, I did it and I wasn't eight feet tall (more like five feet seven) and was rarely mad at anyone.

So the notion grew in me that other people might be interested in knowing how an ordinary mortal, a generally peaceable midwestern American, managed to get into and out of the clutches of a ruthless and efficient enemy. And how I and other lucky ones fared in Switzerland, until it was possible to escape friendly captivity and get back to the war.

Although my adventure was extraordinary, I was not an extraordinary young man. I was a farm boy from Indiana who happened to be at the right age and reasonably fit when the war came along. At Manchester College in Indiana during the critical years 1936–1940, amid the smug security of the Chicago Tribune isolationist preserve, I watched the madness take over in Europe. I was a good student during the first three years, but in my last year I couldn't see much point in studying: I was certain that the United States would have to go to war, in which event I would too.

Manchester was and is a college of the Church of the Brethren, one of the "Churches for Peace." Most of my acquaintances were pacifists, and in due course all but a few of my closest friends became conscientious objectors. I found the pacifist arguments persuasive but, ultimately, not convincing. Most important, however, was my consuming curiosity about the war; it was too vital a human drama to miss. Avoid the most gigantic rhubarb in the history of man? Me? Not likely!

So in the summer and fall of 1940, a year before the Japanese attack on Pearl Harbor catapulted the United States into war, I tried three times to pass the exacting test for Air Corps pilot training, and was rejected each time. After my third failure I was told not to apply again.

In February 1941 I was drafted and wound up as a rifleman in the 2d Infantry Regiment, 5th Division, at Fort Custer, Michigan, resigned to the prospect of seeing the war through the sights of an M-1 rifle. But when they transferred me to the regimental band and issued me a clarinet in place of the rifle, I thought the hell with it and risked a fourth try for pilot training. This time I skinned through.

I had my primary training at Sikeston, Missouri, then basic and advanced training at Randolph Field and Brooks Field, both near San Antonio, Texas. On March 7, 1942, I became an officer, a gentleman, and a pilot. I was not a "natural-born flier," and though I'm still not sure I know what gets the machine up and keeps it there, in time I became a very good airplane driver.

Shortly after my graduation I was assigned to an observation squadron (very soon to be redesignated tactical reconnaissance) based at El Paso, whose mission was to patrol the Texas-Mexican border. The flight I was to work with was operating out of a field near Laredo. It was there that I turned around one evening at a dance and looked into the eyes of the most enchanting creature I had ever seen. In the midst of our courtship I was transferred to Alexandria, Louisiana, to a group that was staging to go overseas. But Mary Lee came there and we were married in August 1942. Three weeks later I shipped out with my squadron to England.

In those days there appeared to be two widely divergent assessments of my character and personality. For my part, I had always thought of myself as contemplative and of a philosophical turn of mind, a student and in time possibly a scholar. I read Huxley and Korzybski (my crowd at Manchester was much taken with general semantics), and given a choice I preferred Beethoven and Mozart to Glenn Miller and Benny Goodman. Admittedly I was given to bursts of exuberance (one of which led to a general court martial), and I never let a good book get in the way of a crap game or a squadron brawl. But if anyone had troubled to ask me, I would have characterized myself as a somewhat sensitive introvert.

My buddies in the outfit had me sized up differently. For example, a paragraph in the official squadron journal describes the circumstances of my being shot down (I was the first in the 67th Group to go down over enemy territory) and then goes on to say, "Hickman was recognized as one of the squadron's outstanding pilots, a crazy, daredevil kid who surprised everyone by the thoroughness of his work. Though no word has come of him yet, there is no doubt that any day he will come walking into camp with a whale of a story."

When I got back to the squadron after my unofficial tour of the continent, I asked "No-No" Anderson, our intelligence officer, how the gang had reacted to the news of my bail-out.

"About like you'd expect," the captain replied. "I met your wingman Kile on the line when he landed, and got the story for my intelligence report, then we drove up to the mess and broke the news. Everybody who knew you figured you would make out okay, and beyond that I guess Johnny Hoefker's remark about summed up our feelings. He said in that Kentucky drawl of his, 'The ornery little bastard couldn't wait for the invasion like the rest of us—he had to go in and tackle them single-handed!' "

PART ONE

Germans and Assorted Frenchmen

1

Kile swung his plane into position off my right wing and acknowledged radio contact with a wave of his hand. I switched to fighter control.

"Redhead from Gluepot Purple One. We are airborne and on course. Do you read me? Over." A crisp English voice came back immediately, "Gluepot Purple One from Redhead, you are loud and clear. Listening out."

I lined out at treetop level for Beachy Head, on England's south coast. We would stay low as possible, even over land, to avoid the sweep of German radar. For some twenty minutes we skimmed over the lovely rolling Hampshire and Sussex landscapes, dotted with picture-postcard cottages. Instruments, fuel, and headings plotted on the pad strapped to my thigh checked OK. It was an auspicious start for what was to be my last combat mission of the war.

We sped up over a grassy hill and down the other side, and abruptly we were at the coast, Beachy Head right over the Mustang's slim nose and Eastbourne on up the coast to the left. I changed course slightly, flipped on the gun switch, and swung down low over the thrashing gray waves. Soon Beachy Head and the entire coast were lost in the thick channel air.

Lt. Richard Kile, my wingman, and I had eaten an early supper and suited up for the flight in the deserted ready room, with only the intelligence officer for company. But it was early May, and already the days were long, so it would still be daylight when we returned within the next couple of hours. The rest of the pilots and ground crew had long since left for the day, and the dispersal area was deserted except for the few men required to get us on our way.

My crew chief helped strap me in the cockpit, and he reminded me to check the plane's speed. The two of us had spent the past three days cleaning and waxing the entire outer skin of the plane in order to add a few miles an hour to its speed. AX-P was the brightest and cleanest flying machine in the squadron, and we were anxious to see how much the plane's performance improved as a result of our work.

The 107th Squadron of the 67th Group, 9th Air Force, was a tactical reconnaissance outfit flying armed, camera-equipped single-seater P-51s (Mustangs). For the past three days we had been running a series of visual reconnaissance missions over western France to observe what visible reactions the Germans might have shown to the mammoth day-run invasion exercise, Operation Fabius, the Allies had mounted in the channel the last of April. Kile and I were flying the last of this series of surveillance missions. We were to fly inland from the little French coastal town of Le Touquet to Saint-Pol, a distance of about forty miles, then south another forty and head for home. It was a round trip from takeoff to landing of about two hours. The morning and afternoon flights, like the ones before, had reported no activity on the ground and encountered very little flak and no enemy air opposition.

"It'll be a cinch, Hickman," Captain Anderson had said. "Probably won't even see flak, since all the Krauts'll be eating supper." Just as he turned to leave the ready room, he added, "But now that I've told you that, the goddam Germans will probably make a liar out of me."

A few miles off the French coast, with my landfall ahead and slightly to the left, I signaled Kile and we put on power to climb steeply into the clear evening sky. As we climbed, I listened for the pulsing background sound that the German radar put into the headset, and when it came, the sound of it tightened my stomach. The sky over enemy territory always looked vast and menacing, and the ever-present *zzummzzumm* of radar impulses gave me that uneasy feeling of being watched.

At ten thousand feet and on course for Saint-Pol, I called fighter control again, reported landfall, and asked if there was any news. The clipped accents replied, "Gluepot Purple One from Redhead. There is no enemy air activity in your vicinity. Listening out." It was some comfort to realize that our own people were watching us too.

This was a routine mission, and we were as usual two planes, two pilots. I concentrated on the ground, watching roads and fields for signs of military activity while Kile swung widely to and fro, watching for enemy aircraft. One thing was different about this flight, however. The week before, I had returned from a mission over Paris with only five gallons of fuel in my tanks because of too much cloud in the wrong place and too much wind from the wrong quarter. So on this "milk run" I was experimenting with minimum power settings to save fuel: lean fuel mixture, low operating RPM, and moderate throttle setting.

Maybe that made a difference in what followed, but maybe not. We were about twenty-five miles inland from the coast, and although it was still bright daylight up where we were, it was dusk on the ground. I spotted two trucks moving along the main road toward the coast, so I called Kile to tell him I was going down for a look-see and maybe make a strafing pass.

He circled at altitude and I started down in an easy, wide turn to the left, keeping the trucks in sight over my left wing. It was hard to make out much detail in the twilight, so I was down to about twenty-five hundred feet in a fast, steep turn before I could see that these were civilian trucks with no military markings. I was now headed south, and I straightened out of my turn, pulled up the nose of the plane, and started an easy climb back upstairs.

And the blue evening exploded into a shuddering, banging bedlam. Someone had hit my plane with a huge baseball bat, and I instinctively broke sharp left, thinking there was an enemy plane behind me doing all the shooting. When I recovered my senses the plane was in a racking, too-tight turn to the left and I was craning back to see where the pursuing ME-109 was, wondering numbly why my Mustang hadn't gone to pieces. I turned my face forward again and saw that it was my own guns that were firing. I had frozen on the control stick trigger and my four guns were spraying .50-caliber slugs all over the sky.

Fully recovered from my momentary panic, I realized that my plane was about to stall in with only partial power on, so I jammed the stick forward, kicked right rudder, and pushed throttle, fuel mixture, and prop control to full war power. I was suddenly aware of the flak filling the sky—red tracers converging lazily on my plane from scores of dancing red fires on the ground, and large black flowers blossoming all about me.

I felt a wave of shame at having gone into a panic, but with my plane righted, my shame changed quickly to a flaring anger at what those bastards down there had done to me. I pushed the Mustang's nose down, and with my engine straining wildly I singled out the first flak position I saw and slanted steeply straight at it, firing as soon as I was lined out, watching my tracers mingle with those arching up toward me. I pushed home my kamikaze attack and quit firing only when I saw bodies flung about as my bullet pattern found them, and I saw the brace of guns quit firing and swing away crazily.

As I swung low over the gun position and started sharply upward again, my anger drained away and left me with the worry about climbing out of reach of that deadly web of flak. Automatically and for the first time since the start of this brief aeon of action, I looked at my instrument panel. It was another space of time before the wreckage of the upper part of the panel made me realize, fully and palpably, that my plane *had* been hit. My first reaction was surprise. There were my navigation instruments all shattered and a jagged hole at the top of the panel, as though someone had jammed a rail through it, probably from below. My next move was automatic: I moved both legs and wiggled my feet. I was intact.

This all took place as I was climbing back after strafing the gun position, and with full power I was weaving and climbing through those searching tracers. The whole episode probably lasted less than forty-five seconds, from the hit to the stall, then through the strafing pass and the beginning of the climb.

I was back up to about two thousand feet when Kile called, "Hey, Hickman, flak!" And immediately: "I think you're hit!"

I looked at the engine gauge instruments at the bottom right-hand side of the instrument panel; the single clockface that registered oil and engine coolant temperatures and oil pressure was undamaged, but what it told me clamped a cold hand on my bowels. The engine temperature needle was as far into red as it could go, and beginning to drift back; the oil temperature was extreme; and no oil pressure registered. I had been hit in that soft underbelly of the P-51, the coolant and oil radiator, located under and behind the cockpit. With no oil and no coolant, my mind told me, I had three to five minutes of engine left. A fleeting regret swept over me with the realization that I was cut off from my familiar life as surely as if I were dead. I had to force myself to think and do the things I knew had to be done, but my mouth was full of cotton; there was an unreality about the whole proceeding.

First I reduced power in order to nurse my engine. I was now at about three thousand feet, still taking evasive action. Next I headed in a general southerly direction, the idea being to get as close to Spain and freedom as possible. This was a measure of my clarity, since Spain was five hundred miles away.

I had already accepted that my engine would quit soon, so I had to decide whether to make a crash-landing or bail out. I had always thought that my best bet would be to crash-land rather than to parachute, but as I looked down at all those guns spitting red in the dusk, I knew that a landing attempt would be suicide, that I must get the hell out the hard way.

That settled, I called Kile, and in a voice I controlled only by effort I told him I was going to bail out, asked him if he knew his safe course home, and told him to stick around until I had hit the ground. He acknowledged, and said he had his heading for England.

Next, jettison the canopy. The cold blast of air increased my sense of fateful separation from things known. Then throw away my flight helmet, since I had been warned of the danger of becoming tangled in the headset radio cords during bail-out. My throat was parched, and overlaying this ritual of chaos was the conviction that it couldn't be so, it just couldn't be!

Set the trim nose-heavy, so on my back the plane will pull upward and away as I drop out. By this time the engine was running rough, but still putting out power. OK, roll her over. On my back, I looked toward the ground and couldn't force myself to pull the harness release lever, so I sloughed upright again, sweat streaming down my neck, left hand still on the throttle, and right hand choking the stick. More evasive action as I continued the climb, the flak still thick. More altitude would be to my advantage.

Suddenly the prop ground to a stop as the overheated engine tore its moving parts to pieces in noisy agony. That cut the string, so I turned the plane over again and pulled the harness release.

2

At the moment I pulled the harness release I was in a fixed position with respect to earth, sky, and motion, frightened but still in a right relationship with familiar things. The next instant, with no transition, I was torn by a great wind in a place of no sky, no earth, and no gravity, just me and a hurricane.

Those few seconds of free fall were remarkable mostly because of the sensation of weightlessness, with nothing of the fearful falling sensation one has when looking down from a high window. I felt no fear, only a small wonder at the immense wind. I even drew myself up in a ball and extended an arm to see if it would make any difference in the way the wind struck me.

I gave no thought to my rip cord until the wind abated, until I had lost most of the two-hundred-mile-an-hour forward momentum I had when I fell out of the plane. There was a steady, perceptible lessening of the flailing wind, and somewhere in my mind there was remembrance of an instruction, because at a point determined by God knows what meshing of judgment and instinct, I jerked the rip cord.

The wind briefly continued to roar, and then I felt a jerk—a sensation more mental than physical—and earth and sky snapped into clear, placid relationship with me, god-like, surveying. This was just as my childhood dreams had pictured flying: quiet, buoyant, drifting. After the tumult of the past few minutes, I was flooded with a wonderful serenity, at peace with this deepening evening.

I looked up at the taut, white pattern of my chute against the blue sky and marveled at its geometrical perfection. I looked off to my left just in time to see my plane in full silhouette dive swiftly, perpendicular to the earth, and disappear in a billow of orange flame.

A stuttering racket shattered the evening and froze my blood. As I grabbed the shroud lines, half in a gesture of surrender and half to start my body swinging, I thought frantically, "Those dirty bastards are shooting at me!"

My eyes found them, then, a brace of guns on the ground chattering intermittently, the tracers arching away to the north. They were firing at Kile.

The closeness of the guns dragged my distracted senses back to the problem of landing. At maybe two hundred feet, I was close enough to the ground to sense my rate of descent, and I could see I was drifting well over a fence at the near end of an open field, with a patch of woods to my left. At the far end of this little field was a hedged road, and beyond it an orchard. There was a cluster of tree-shaded buildings some hundreds of yards to the right of the orchard.

Fearing to drift into the orchard ahead of me, I dumped my chute slightly to cut the angle of glide, but then the onrushing ground told me landing was the immediate problem and I knew I would land in open ground. From a briefing by a paratrooper weeks before, the admonition crossed my mind: feet together, knees slightly bent, hands up on the two shroud risers, and eyes on the horizon. But I was unable to decide whether the nearest union of sky and earth was the horizon or whether it was somewhat more in the distance. In the midst of this quandary, I hit the ground; but I can't recall the hitting, only the tumbling over, getting to my knees, spilling the chute, and fumbling with the chute harness.

As I unbuckled the harness, my breath was fast and my heart was hammering. I was still unable to grasp the enormity that here I was, in enemy country, a fugitive. The thing I had dreaded, had nightmares about, had happened. I knew I had to act, had to get away, but the feeling persisted that this was a ridiculous storybook situation; it couldn't happen to a real person.

I took off my knee pad, since it had slipped down to my ankle and knocked against my shin when I moved. In my desperate haste it seemed an endless task, but I got it off. I had just started for the woods when I realized that my chute, glowing white in the dusk, should be gotten out of sight, so I gathered it up in my arms and ran for the woods.

I stopped at the edge of the woods, stuffed the chute and my Mae West behind some bushes, tore off the top sheets from my knee pad and put them into my pocket, then started running into the woods. Now I had to hide myself.

So I blundered and tore through the light brush and was suddenly on the other side of the copse, looking out into an open field. Back again I went, found some thick brush, and hid in it. As I settled down, I realized that I was only a few feet from a path and only a little way in from where I'd first entered the trees. So I moved again, and this time found a brush pile in a thick part of the woods and covered myself in it. As I lay there I recalled all the wood lore my mind could lay on to and acted accordingly. I rubbed dirt on my face so it wouldn't show light in the gathering darkness and did the same with my yellow horsehide gloves. Then I took the crumpled sheets I'd torn from my knee pad and buried them. They showed our takeoff point, our course, and other information the enemy should not have.

Finally there was nothing to do but wait, and a vast, charged silence encompassed the world. I don't know how long that silence lasted, perhaps five minutes, but I can recall vivid impressions: the smell of forest mold, a dog barking in the distance (barking in French, I thought), the vast jumbled wilderness of boulders and rotten timbers three inches from my nose, and the hammering of my heart. I set about deliberately to control that beating by breathing deeply and regularly, and relaxing all my muscles. It worked; I was almost calm.

Suddenly there was a voice calling softly from the direction I had first entered the woods, *"Américain! Américain!"* With my heart thumping again, I debated risking an answer, but rejected the idea. The Germans had seemed so close by, and by this time, this eternity, must surely be at hand. Maybe it was a trick to lure me out. So I lay still and heard the call repeated, then silence.

By now there was only a lingering light, and I was feeling that there would probably be no search. But just as I was relaxing again I heard them, tramping into the underbrush at the far edge of the trees. There were two voices, calling to each other as they came closer and closer to my hiding place. Pictures of burly soldiers with rifles at ready loomed up in my mind, and for the first time in my adult life I experienced the overwhelming terror of the hunted. I, who had an imperfect understanding of violence, even war's violence, cowered under a miserable heap of forest trash in an unnamed place in a strange land, hunted by men with guns.

One of the men tramped within ten feet of my hiding place. I saw his boots but didn't dare to raise my eyes higher. He stopped and called, "Hans! *Komm!*" Then he clumped away, and soon I was alone again with the darkness and the night sounds of an alien land.

I lay there for a long time, perhaps two hours, then got up and sat with my back to a tree to think what to do. I lit a cigarette, and for the first time since my plane was hit, I thought of my wife and family. But I could make no progress in that direction; they were too hopelessly disconnected from the present. I felt a great longing, however, to be back with my squadron. How utterly desirable it seemed then to be experiencing the humdrum sequences of an evening at the base: a mediocre dinner, Frank Dillon's pragmatic humor, a pint of beer and a Bob Hope movie, a late snack of eggs fried in a mess kit over our coke fire. How easy it could have been, just an hour's flight. And here I sat, alone and hunted, cut off from the life I knew as surely as though I were on the moon.

I took stock. I had the standard assortment of emergency

equipment, all done up in a small plastic box that fit into
my breast pocket. It included a compass, a rubber water
bottle, a map of France printed on silk, an assortment of
pills to purify water and to keep a person awake, and six
cigarettes and some matches. In addition to the escape kit I
had a GI wristwatch, a little compass no bigger than the
end of a finger, and a pocket-sized toilet kit I'd put together
for use when I might be kept at a strange base overnight.

The immediate question was what to do next. I was
completely unequipped psychologically for this game I was
playing and wished intensely I didn't have to go on. My
reluctance to face the ugly facts produced a paralyzing
lethargy, but I had to do *something*.

What first? Briefing officers had told us to get as far
away from the landing spot as possible the first night. So
that was it: Move—any direction, but move. I'd wait, I
thought, until midnight and then start traveling.

I waited the interval I'd allotted myself, then crept as
quietly as I could to the edge of the wood, and realized, as
I looked across the pasture field, that traveling by night
was going to be quite a problem. I would have to keep in
shadow, because open spaces would expose me. A full
moon in a clear sky made the world bright.

I crept along the edge of the wood toward the lower end
of the pasture, where I found a road deeply sunk between
rampartlike hedges. I skirted along this road to the woods a
quarter of a mile across the pasture from where I was
hiding, and started back up the slope, along what appeared
to be a wagon track. As I neared the squared end of this
patch of trees, where the tracks turned left, I stopped at the
back end of a truck. Truck, I thought—that means soldiers,
enemy soldiers. I immediately succeeded in convincing myself that this was an enemy truck (it probably wasn't), and
retreated from it.

The night no longer seemed to be my friendly ally,
darkness covering my retreat, with a full moon lighting me
on. Now it was a dread camouflage concealing all sorts of
traps, and the moonlight conspired with obscure shapes to
trick me into imagining huge men in every corner, guns and

trucks and hutments at every turn. What composure I had built up during my wait in the woods left me, and I went onward with a pounding heart and a dry mouth.

I did not know for sure that what I thought I saw was really there, but I felt trapped in what seemed a quarter-mile square, with the road running through the center. I kept in the shadows, to the edge of the wood patches, the orchard, the hedges; and the more intensely alert I became, the more it seemed that everywhere I turned there was an encampment, a cluster of trucks, a gun position, or sentries talking softly in the spring night. I was sure my senses were playing tricks on me. There simply couldn't be that many Germans in France!

When I rejoined my squadron months later, I learned that there *were* that many Germans, at least in certain parts of France. I had landed smack on the defense perimeter of a robot-bomb launching site, one of the many heavily defended areas from which the Germans, within six weeks, were to begin launching the deadly V-1 robot-bombs against England. Besides the installation housing the launching equipment itself, each of these sites included a surrounding network of antiaircraft positions covering an area of about a square mile around the site. Outside of landing in the center of a large town, I could not have come down in a worse place.

In my groping about I had come to realize that there was a village just around the bend of my road, and as I sat resting in the orchard near the road, I debated whether or not to walk through the village. I reasoned that in the dark I would not be conspicuous among the inhabitants and could probably get through to what seemed, to my fevered mind, to be the safety of "the other side." What did not occur to me was the obvious fact that in a country village anyone would be conspicuous walking about at 2 A.M., especially with a curfew in force in a restricted *Festung Europa*, and an American pilot known to be somewhere around.

But the idea took hold, so I started walking toward the village. The road swung sharply to the left, along some low stone buildings, putting me in shadow. I toyed with the idea of hiding in a broken-down stable there so I could size things up by daylight, but the compulsion to move along was too strong.

The road continued in this direction for perhaps fifty yards, then turned full right around the corner of a cottage. I stepped out of the shadow with the turn, and felt my scalp begin to tingle before I was aware of what was wrong. By then it was too late to do anything about it without appearing furtive. I was walking up this village street in the full, revealing glare of the moonlight.

3

I'd blundered! And as the hair prickled at the back of my neck, I knew I must get off to the side, into darkness. Then I heard voices, not thirty yards ahead of me, and saw the dim shapes of men, two of them, one on each side of the road, in shadow. There was no ducking out now. I had to bluff through. I tried to make myself appear as French as possible and even whistled a French nursery tune.

My play lasted only a few moments. Shortly these men came out of the shadows, rifles at ready, the moon glinting on pot helmets so familiar on movie Germans. A word was spoken to me, and I ventured a querulous, *"Q'est-ce que c'est?"* The speaker, now closer, then said something I understood: *"Hände hoch!"* I put up my hands and repeated my French with less hope, and knew the jig was up when I heard one say to the other, *"Amerikaner!"*

The helmeted soldiers came forward, guns aimed at me. They halted a few yards away, and conferred briefly; then, while one of them kept me covered, the other stepped forward and felt around my chest and waist to see if I carried a weapon.

Satisfied, they motioned me down the road in the direction from which they had come, making it clear that I was to keep my hands up. So there I was, an adult playing a game I had outgrown when I was twelve, walking down a brightly moonlit street at two o'clock in the morning, hands above my head, with two armed strangers in movie costumes walking behind me, talking in an alien tongue.

We walked through the village for some fifteen minutes. When my arms got tired, the Germans permitted me to lace my fingers together and rest my hands on top of my head. At last we turned into a gateway and walked a hundred yards up a gravel driveway to a large villa. I was ushered into an entryway and directed to the right into a dimly lighted room that appeared to be guards' quarters. A stove stood in the middle of the room; a rack for rifles and gear was mounted on the far wall. To my left, at the dim end of the room, were half a dozen double-decker bunks.

One of my captors set a chair under the light and directed me to sit down. The other spoke at some length into a telephone while the first one talked to a collecting group of half-dressed, curious soldiers roused from their bunks by the important-sounding noises being fed into the phone.

We examined one another silently but with mutual curiosity, the enemy and I, and they showed no more hostility toward me than I felt toward them. During this examination period, I remembered occasionally to scowl, and finally I stretched out my legs, jammed my hands into my pockets, and said "Shit!"

The gathering group laughed, and looking at them I had to smile. They were familiar faces. But for the uniforms and the language, they might have been a group of farm boys from Union Township back in Indiana. In their various stages of undress, they had about them none of the formidable look they were supposed to have. And not being one to buck the odds, I followed my natural Hoosier inclination to relax and get acquainted.

I hauled out a crumpled pack of cigarettes and offered them around. The soldiers gave me my first surprise. They not only would not accept my offer of cigarettes, they would not let me smoke one of my own, but gave me one of theirs. They made me understand that I should hoard mine. One of the men brought me a thermos of cold tea, and in a combination of German, French, and English conveyed that the water was not safe, and that I should drink only tea made from boiled water as long as I was in France.

The ice was broken, and the men began asking me questions: rank, age; was I married and did I have children. I showed them the pictures of my wife, my parents, and my brothers, a little collection I always carried in my shirt pocket, and after that the men were downright friendly. It was a valuable lesson, the effect of this little family album on strangers. Wherever I went, my portable portrait gallery did me more good than anything else I could have carried.

Another thing that struck me as curious was the frequently repeated congratulation that amounted to, "You are lucky—for you the war is finished!" They seemed genuinely happy for me, and a bit envious, that I was out of the shooting and safely a prisoner.

In this friendly company, I learned a thing that spared me some trouble later. These men knew I was a flier, but it made a difference what kind of flier I was. I had a pretty good grasp of French and knew quite a few words of German, but I couldn't catch on to one line of questioning. The terms, often repeated in both French and German, distinguished between a fighter plane and a bomber. The importance of the distinction came home to me only when they pushed one of their number forward and said "Hamburg!" and gestured destruction from the sky. I got the drift, and with my fingernail drew on the table a crude outline of a fighter plane, making a point of the single engine. They were pleased that I was identified as a *chasseur* or a *Flieger* rather than as one engaged in dropping bombs on German cities.

This stumbling conversation went on for about an hour, and my hosts seemed not at all put out when, in response to such a question as where my base was, or where I came from in America, I replied, *"Nicht verstehen,"* "I don't understand." They showed me pieces of their equipment, handed me one of the heavy pot helmets to try on, and even let me examine a rifle, emptied carefully first.

One of them also showed me an empty shell case, something in size between our .50 caliber machine gun bullet and our 20 millimeter cannon shell, and gave me to understand that that was what had brought me down. Two of the men also asserted that I had killed six soldiers in my strafing pass.

I was beginning to feel a bit tired when a new fellow entered the room, a noncommissioned officer about my size, a hard-looking character. He directed me to print my name on a paper he gave me, then proceeded to search me. I emptied my pockets, then had to unbutton my shirt and remove the talisman I wore loosely tied around my neck— one of my wife's stockings, holding her lipstick and a shilling in the toe. I'd picked up the notion from a French fighter pilot, Bob Goubey, whose wing I had flown several times during a short assignment with the British RAF 165 Squadron. Goubey was a handsome, dashing fellow, wild as heather, with twelve victories in his logbook. His particular rabbit's foot was the stocking-lipstick-coin bit, which struck my fancy. I wrote my wife and had her send me the stocking and the lipstick, and from that time on I wore the talisman constantly, until the Germans took it away from me. This bit of sentimental jingoism made quite an impression on the German boys.

The sergeant tried to explain something to me, but I couldn't follow. So he put all my possessions, which included my escape kit, watch, and pocket compass, into a little bag, which he turned over to the fellow apparently charged with guarding me. He let me keep my pictures and all my silver coins, about four dollars' worth of shillings, half crowns, and sixpence pieces, but took away my paper money and my talisman in spite of arguments from his fellow Germans. His search had overlooked my trousers watch pocket, so I still kept the pea-sized compass.

He then indicated that we were going to leave, patted his machine pistol, and made another stern little speech. One of the soldiers who had a few words of English explained the instruction: "You run, he shoot." I nodded that I understood, and we filed out into the night. In the drive stood a small pickup truck with a canvas top over the rear.

Two soldiers with rifles got in back with me, and the fly was laced into place. The sergeant then got into the cab with the driver, and we were off.

We traveled for about fifteen minutes, stopped, and all got out. A very low concrete building hunkered close by, distinct in the now waning moonlight; with a quick look around I saw no other structures. We went immediately down a flight of stairs to a door on this low building, its flat top only a few feet above the ground, and entered a dim corridor; the walls and ceiling were of unfinished concrete. Some more soldiers were here; they only stared at me. After my sergeant spoke to one of them, I was shown to a cage made of rough wood and heavy wire screen and furnished with a chair and a crude bed with a straw mattress and some blankets.

By now I was dead tired. It must have been close to 4 A.M., and I'd had a busy day, so I loosened my shoe buckles and collar and got ready to lie down. Then I noticed the tall blond soldier who stood just outside my open door, staring at me. He had evidently been there awhile, and he made no move to go away even though I obviously was preparing to sleep. His stare was persistent yet preoccupied, as though he were trying to fit what he saw into some pattern in his mind. Although there was no hatred on his face, neither was there any sign of the human interest I had seen on the faces of the first group of soldiers I had met. The effect was unnerving; he was like a zombie. He didn't budge when I waved a dismissive hand at him and said, *"Raus!"* One of the other men came over and spoke to him, and he turned on his heel and left. I fell immediately into a sound and dreamless sleep.

A soldier roused me around the middle of the morning and handed me a large mug of hot fluid, which he said was coffee. It wasn't coffee, but it was hot and pungent, so I drank the stuff, and felt considerably better for it.

Then I set about making myself presentable and comfortable. My clothing was good. I was wearing GI shorts and a light wool, short-sleeved undershirt; a heavy khaki shirt; regulation dark green trousers; a battle-dress jacket of my own design with a chamois leather lining covered with silk; solid, well-made paratrooper boots; and heavy wool socks. These socks were by now sticky-dirty, and they bothered me. All things considered, however, I was pretty well off as far as clothing was concerned. I had even been allowed to keep my horsehide gloves, so except for a cap, I was practically regulation. While in the woods, before my capture, I had taken off my insignia of rank and put the bars in my pocket. Now I put them back on.

While I was still in my cell, I transferred my tiny compass from my watch pocket into the little finger of my left glove. Although this bit of my personal escape gear had been overlooked in the first search of my person, I was certain a much more thorough search would be made later. I figured that by careful handling of my gloves I might work them past a search and so have at least a compass should I manage somehow to escape.

I shook my clothing free of visible dirt, wiped my shoes on one of the blankets, and turned attention to getting my hands and face clean. My face particularly needed a wash, since it still carried much of the dirt I had rubbed on it in the woods. I asked for my toilet kit, but the guard could not or would not understand what I was asking for. He did bring me a small pan of water, so with my handkerchief I managed to clean off the worst of the soil.

A soldier came and beckoned me to follow him. Well, I thought, the prisoner is now marched off for questioning. From our briefings on German interrogation methods, I expected a heavy guard and a considerable show of brusqueness during this initial period. The idea was to build up the prisoner's sense of aloneness so that later a sympathetic and congenial interrogating officer would make the prisoner feel inclined to cooperate with him.

When I went out of the building into the sunlight of a faultless May morning, I looked around expectantly for the armored car that would take me the next lap of my trip. But there was no armored car. I was ordered instead into the back end of a canvas-topped truck about the size of our own army six-by-sixes. The truck bed was piled high with bags of laundry, and lounging on the heap, up toward the front, were two people. One was a soldier armed with a rifle, which he held across his lap and kept pointed in my direction, and the other was a buxom, pleasant-faced girl wearing a baggy, nondescript uniform. They looked me over silently, listened to the words of the soldier who had escorted me out of the building, then resumed their conversation, ignoring me completely—except that the man kept the rifle pointed at me. So the prisoner of war was to be hauled away along with the detachment's dirty clothing, guarded by the laundry clerk and his doxy. Hell!

4

The truck engine coughed to life, we bounded out onto a main road, and I was seeing France from the ground in daylight for the first time in my life, from the open rear of a German army laundry truck.

It was a beautiful spring day. As we rode along, I made myself comfortable amid the laundry bags and speculated about my future. I knew I had no further responsibility in determining what was to become of me, and the thought was accompanied by a feeling of deliverance. It was the familiar freedom from worry about the basic personal decisions; I had come to recognize it long before as one of the attractive aspects of military life. A man on his own is accountable to himself for how he uses, or fails to use, his talents and his time, and for providing for his own needs (and maybe others' too). Draft that man into the military service, and he is no longer responsible for the shape of his destiny. The knowledge is a profound relief, though it carries with it a nagging fragment of worry that it is wrong to feel good about such a circumstance.

I learned one thing that surprised me in the course of this morning ride. On our reconnaissance missions over France, this very part of France, we had always been on the look-out for German planes. It was the dearest hope of each pilot in the group to make the first kill. But I—and, I suppose, the others—had continually searched the surrounding sky for Jerries, looking to the ground only for reconnaissance targets (rocket-launching sites, marshaling yards, and troop concentrations). During my seventeen missions I had seen not a single enemy plane over that part of France, and assumed that there simply weren't any there.

During my morning ride, however, I counted at least eight planes: three Stuka dive bombers, two JU-52 cargo planes, and several fighters, all flying close to the deck and well camouflaged. Enemy planes had been there all right, but I had looked in the wrong places for them. My squadron buddy Johnny Hoefker would make the same discovery while he was in a position to do something about it, and manage to run up an impressive score.

Sometime before noon the laundry truck came to a halt in a little town (Hesdin, I learned later), and I was ordered to dismount. They led me through a gate posted with a sentry, and ushered me into an orderly room in a rambling, one-story building. The room was about fifteen by twenty feet, with the entry on one of the narrow ends. Opposite the door, against the far wall, was a desk facing into the room, which I later found was usually occupied by the noncommissioned officer in charge. Just to the right of the desk was a door to a back room, and beside this door was a rack on which rifles, helmets, and other gear not in use were kept neatly arranged.

Against the long wall to the right of a person entering was a smaller desk with a field telephone and a typewriter on it, and centered against that wall was a potbellied heating stove. Set into the wall opposite the stove were two windows that looked out onto the street, and between the windows was a table and a chair—my dining table and post of observation. A straw-filled mattress—my bed—was spread on the floor each night in the corner to the left of the main door.

When I was brought in, I was told to sit down at the chair by the table, and from then on I was officially ignored, left to my own devices.

I still hadn't decided how I should behave toward my

captors. I could not feel, and so could not show, contempt for these men—they were impressive. I felt no hatred toward them. And being curious by nature, I couldn't ignore them; I wanted to see how they behaved. So lacking any American equivalent of Bushido, I again followed my natural inclination toward congeniality.

Lunch was a large bowl of thick cabbage-and-potato soup with a chunk of heavy brown bread on the side. There was also a cup of hot "coffee." Although I had gotten worse-looking stuff in our officers' mess back at Middle Wallop, I made a mild protest to the man who set the stuff before me, pointing out that I was an officer and deserved better. An elderly, balding soldier came forward and explained in American English that this was standard fare for all of them, and if I was to eat anything, that would have to do. I ate it.

My English-speaking guard disappeared into the back room for a couple of hours. After lunch, two of the various soldiers who lounged in and out of the main room came over to me and started talking German. They seemed to be asking for something, but I couldn't understand them. They came over again later with the bald one, who told me the men wanted souvenirs. I was low on smokes, so after discussion I got nearly twenty cigarettes in return for two silver coins. I asked if there were any other soldiers who might want to sell me cigarettes, but was told that the tobacco ration was small and most men wanted to keep theirs.

The English-speaking soldier, though he was not inclined to be friendly, did seem willing to talk, so I passed some time in conversation with him. He told me that in 1922 he had gone to the United States to live and had worked in my home state, in factories in Gary and South Bend, for eight or nine years. He had returned to Germany in the early thirties, and had two sons fighting the Russians on the eastern front. It looked as though I had in this man a useful device for satisfying some of my questions about the activities around me. Our friendship, however, was killed aborning by an impertinence on my part that afternoon.

During my first few hours in those quarters, the air raid sirens sounded three times. Each time there would be a bustle as the field phone and some other equipment were carried outside to a bomb shelter; each time I looked on grinning like Cheshire cat. The all clear would sound within ten minutes or so, and everything would be put to rights.

From the first, I noticed that about five minutes after the all clear, the snarling sound of Focke-Wolf fighter engines could be heard overhead, but close to the ground. Late in the afternoon, after about the sixth air raid performance, I asked my baldheaded friend why it was that German fighters put in an appearance only after the all clear, when the aircraft to be intercepted were long gone. He took my question in the spirit in which it was intended and would have no more truck with me.

Notwithstanding such gibes, I was very much impressed by the behavior, high morale, and appearance of these soldiers. They were in the antiaircraft branch, which was part of the Luftwaffe. The men all handled their weapons well and deported themselves in their handsome uniforms with what our technical manuals call "soldierly bearing," something I had not encountered since leaving Randolph Field. The feeling grew in me, and was reinforced by later observation, that if what I was seeing was typical of the entire German army, that army would be hard to beat. I was surprised to learn, and somewhat shaken by the knowledge, that these men did not share my conviction that Germany was losing the war.

The orderly-room routine was also impressive, especially when compared with the more casual atmosphere of the orderly rooms I was familiar with. A soldier coming in from patrol or outside duty would walk over to the desk, where a sergeant or a corporal was always seated, fuss himself into proper position with rifle ordered, then come smartly to attention and make a little speech. He would then go over to the rack and stow his rifle, helmet, and gas mask just so—this orderly room was truly orderly—before going into the back room.

During the first afternoon of my stay there, a soldier

stuck his head in the door and said something that set off a flurry of activity in the room. All but two of the men disappeared into the back room after hurriedly brushing up the floor, and the bald one came over to me and instructed me to stand at attention when the officer came in. I had heard the words *Oberleutnant* spoken, and understood that the officer who was about to grace us with his presence was only a first lieutenant. Thought I to myself, I'm damned if I'll stand even, much less at attention, for a lousy first lieutenant who probably had less time in grade than I did anyway. So I sat sprawled in my chair.

The flurry died down, a redheaded corporal backed off to where he had a good view of the door, and an uneasy suspense filled the room. A step was heard outside the door, the corporal stiffened into a grade A Randolph Field brace and barked *"Achtung!"* and a slight, exceedingly dapper character lounged into the room.

He went over to the desk, sat down, put his beautifully booted feet on the desktop, and began talking to the corporal. The corporal, who had walked over to the desk, stood before it at rigid attention while talking with the officer. Several other men were summoned in turn into The Presence, and they all stood at ramrod attention during their interviews. From my position behind and a little to one side of the men as they talked with the officer, I saw that though they stood at strict attention in front of the officer, while being addressed, when they themselves spoke their fingers straightened stiffly, the gesture lending the impression that the speaker was coming to yet stricter attention.

The questioning completed, the officer lighted a cigarette, gazed out the window awhile in silence, got unhurriedly to his feet, and strolled to the door to the parting *"Achtung"* from the corporal. The whole performance impressed me mightily, and the thought passed through my mind that some of the GIs in our squadron should have been there for a lesson in proper respect for officers. I thought particularly of Sergeant Brodie, a tall, lean, genial crew chief from Mississippi. Only a few days before he had driven me to town in a jeep on an errand. As we parted, Brodie clapped me on the back with his blacksmith's hand and said, "OK, Lootenant, don't fall in no holes. And be back here at nine-thirty!"

Shortly after lunch on May 5, the second day of my captivity, the dapper little *Oberleutnant* showed up again, and in the course of the back-straining and the alien chatter, I became aware that they were talking about me. The officer signed some papers, paused on his way to the door, opposite my chair, and without looking at me pulled his pistol out of its holster, rammed a shell into the chamber, and then stuck the weapon in his waistband. He walked on out, and I was directed by one of the soldiers to follow him.

In the street stood the German equivalent of the American command car, an open vehicle with uncomfortable seats and noisy machinery. I was ordered into the backseat, the bundle containing my worldly goods was put on the floor, and we set off, the officer sitting in the front seat with the driver. This was the end of the casual part of my brief captivity.

5

The prospect of being in a prisoner of war camp didn't bother me. Our intelligence briefings had given me a fair idea of what to expect, so I knew, for example, that as an officer I would not have to work, that I would have access to books, and that I would probably be with other American airmen. Food would be at least adequate. All in all, it was not too bad an outlook. The idea that I might be abused never entered my head. In the course of the morning drive I wondered mainly about how long I would have to be in a POW camp.

We drove for perhaps two hours and finally entered the city of Lille, and came to a halt before a very large old brick-and-stone building. We went in through an arched entryway, and I was led to a kind of reception room, where I could either look out the window or watch the activity immediately about me.

This time all the people were officers, with only an occasional enlisted man slipping deferentially about, and for the first time I became really self-conscious about my appearance. These officers were well dressed, pressed, and greased, but I had neither shaved nor washed properly since the morning of May 3. Now, two and a half days later, I needed a bath.

Here again, I was ignored. No one looked directly at me,

and this disturbing feeling of being completely unimportant was aggravated when a soldier brought in bottles of wine and everyone had a drink but me—the one man there who needed it.

After a tiresome wait I was summoned by a soldier and led up several flights of stairs to a large room full of file cabinets and some long, plain tables. On one of them were laid out the articles that had been taken from me the night I was captured. I guessed that I was to be searched, so I casually laid my gloves, which so far I had been allowed to keep, on one of the other tables. Shortly after I entered the room, I was approached by a middle-aged officer with the look and manner of a college professor. He instructed me in very good English to empty my pockets, then strip down to my shorts. I laid my remaining silver and my collection of family pictures on the table, then proceeded to undress as the officer turned away and left the room.

My clothes were taken by a soldier into another room, and I was left standing, uncomfortably bare, for about fifteen minutes. During this time I noticed three or four officers grouped together across the room, looking at my pictures. I watched, and as I expected, two of them shortly looked over at me, shivering and wretched in my GI shorts, and raised their eyebrows; one fellow whistled softly. They had come across a very good picture of Mary Lee in a bathing suit.

I was a little disappointed in the way these people were handling things, however. They were not asking any questions and were treating me as though they were not much interested in what I might know. I had prepared myself to parry, dramatically and firmly, all sorts of ingenious attempts to get information from me.

Finally my clothes were returned to me, but the rest of my possessions—including my gloves, which one of the soldiers had spotted—were taken away. They allowed me to keep my pictures and identification tags, so I dressed, and for another half hour just sat or wandered around the room. Even though there were half a dozen officers and the same number of enlisted men stirring about, in and out on the Lord only knows what villainous business, the only attention paid me was an occasional annoyed look when I got in someone's way. I even began to feel a bit guilty at just standing around in the midst of all this earnest activity, and once, when I was leaning against a file case that a man wanted to get into, I caught myself murmuring an apology for being in the way.

In his own good time my professorial officer came back into the room and handed me a form, printed in English, which I was to fill out. He explained that it was necessary for the army to have this information so that I could be properly identified and thus be eligible for Red Cross parcels in the prison camp.

I looked the form over and found it to be precisely what I had been told by our intelligence to expect: the Red Cross-parcel ploy.

"I am required to give only my name, rank, and identification number," I said. "This form requests information I am not required to give."

"Your reluctance is understandable," he replied pleasantly, "but it is necessary that you complete this form and sign it if you wish to receive parcels in the prison camp." The officer then adopted a fatherly tone. "This is all a bit new and strange to you, I am sure, and you have no idea how important these parcels are in the camp where you are going. And of course you divulge no military information we do not already have when you answer these questions."

It all seemed quite reasonable, and the questions were such that they seemed to seek only to establish my identity. But we had been repeatedly warned against this very device, so I laid the form on the table and said, "My name is John Forrest Hickman; rank, first lieutenant; serial number, 0-439695."

"You are being impertinent, Lieutenant Hickman," he said testily, "and I have no patience with impertinence. You are a prisoner of war, and you must learn very quickly to do as you are instructed. You will please complete this form with no more foolishness."

He picked up the form and held it out to me, rattling it a

bit for emphasis. This business was beginning to annoy me, so, ignoring the form he was holding under my nose, I said, "Sir, as an officer in an army well known for its discipline, you should be able to understand that I am bound by my orders. And my orders are to give you my name, rank, and serial number and nothing else. I refuse to fill out the form and I refuse to sign it."

I must have raised my voice, because when I was finished I was aware that the others in the room were watching us. There was a moment of silence, and then my antagonist shrugged, turned, and walked away with the form.

Our intelligence briefings had prepared me to expect that the Germans would be correct in their treatment of me. The point had been made time and time again in our instructions that if we were captured and detained by regular German forces, we could demand our rights and expect them to be respected. We were even told of instances in which captured officers, who later escaped and returned to England, had pulled their rank on German noncoms and had gotten away with it. We were advised that in some circumstances a show of arrogance, which the German troops were accustomed to in their own officers, was advisable. My faith in German correctness—a product of theory and cussed optimism—had been fully vindicated; and now that it had been, I felt relieved.

A little while later I was turned over to a wizened little soldier in an oversized uniform. He beckoned and led me away, down a worn stone stairway; through dank, dimly lit passages; through a series of doorways, turnings, and descendings. Down, down, and back into the bowels of this building we went, through a still, flat atmosphere of despair that clung to my spirits like cobwebs. The dread thought grew in my mind that in such a place a person might be shut away from light for endless months, forgotten, in some obscure cell known only to some such mumbling half-wit as shambled before me.

6

Our wandering through this dungeon finally brought us to a heavy wooden door, which Sad Sack unlocked. On the right-hand wall of the room we entered, which was perhaps thirty feet long and twenty wide, were narrow barred windows that looked out onto a stone-paved courtyard. Extending from the other wall were four cells formed of boarding and wire, the partitions running from the floor to the low, vaulted ceiling. Each cell had a padlocked door opening onto the aisle that ran the length of the room, next to the windows.

The jailer walked in ahead of me, unlocked the door to a cell, and motioned me inside. I stood in the doorway and looked into the cell, which was illuminated only by what little light came in through the narrow windows. I saw there a wood-slat bench, a chair, and an uncovered slop pail. A single coarse blanket, neatly folded but obviously not very big, sat on the bench. The cell itself was about six feet wide and ten feet long.

As I was looking the situation over, not quite comprehending that this was the cell I was to be locked up in, the wretched little half-wit tried to push me the rest of the way in by closing the door on me. But I pushed my way out and began protesting. I don't know what I'd been expecting, but the thought of being locked up in that cage was intolerable.

"*Ich bin ein Offizier—das ist nicht für ein Offizier*, you miserable little bastard!" I protested. "*Nein, nein! Verstehensie? Vo* the hell is *die* commanding officer?"

The jailer stood patiently through my mongrel protest, his head a little bowed and wiggling idiotically. When he thought I was through, he motioned me into the cell, but I started up again, determined to get some improvements in the accommodations. I grasped his skinny arm for emphasis, pointed to the blanket, and held up three fingers.

"*Drei, drei!* I need three—*drei*—blankets. *Ich bin Oberleutnant*, goddamit, and I need *ein, zwei, drei*, blankets! *Verstehen?*"

He wagged his head and mumbled "*Nein, nein*," and again motioned me into the cell.

"Why you dumb sonnavabitch German pig! *Nein!* Understand? *Verstehen*, eh? *Ich* will *nicht!* I won't go in, by God!" With this I planted myself firmly in the aisle, folded my arms, and glowered at the sorry little man, encouraged by my surge of righteous indignation.

He peered up at me a moment, the beginnings of anger in his wrinkled face, then turned his head and called out "Karl!" Karl appeared at the door almost immediately, a real, life-sized soldier with a real, life-sized gun. This put a somewhat different light on the matter, so I shrugged and went into the cell. The door banged shut, I heard the lock snap home, and for the first time since my capture the real meaning of the word *prisoner* began to get through to me.

While there was still light, I examined my cell. I tested the wooden bench, my "bed." It was crude, solid, and hard, and a portion at the far end, slanted upward at a thirty-degree angle, was to serve as my pillow. The boards, running crosswise, had spaces between them, and although the edges of the slats were rounded, this feature merely increased the discomfort. I checked the blanket and found it to be considerably smaller and lighter than a U.S. Army blanket, but it smelled fairly clean and there was no livestock pasturing in it that I could detect in the weak light.

Aside from the bench, the crude chair, and the slop pail, the place was bare. Nothing more: four plain walls, a dreary stone ceiling, failing daylight (although it was still late afternoon), and a growing chill in the air. To stop my shivering I began to pace up and down the cell, the blanket wrapped around my shoulders, entertaining a succession of depressing thoughts.

Before I had even gotten around to thinking about food in this dismal dump, I heard the outer door being opened, then my own door unlocked, and my little gaoler edged in with buckets and a pan. He set the pan on the end of my bed, put a chunk of dark bread in it, and on top of that a fish about six inches long. Out of the pail he dipped a large cup of dark fluid, set the cup down, and started out. I realized I was being served dinner!

As the man started out the door, I bawled *"Achtung!"* grabbed him by the arm, pointed at the food he had set there, and went through my officer routine again with my dozen German words and quite a few unprintable English ones. So he would understand, I contemptuously dumped bread, fish, and liquid into the slop pail and tossed the tinware into the aisle. Then I shook a corner of the blanket under his nose and held up three fingers, trying to get the idea across to him again that I wanted more blankets, and hoped my frequent repetition of *"Ich bin Oberleutnant"* would aid his comprehension.

All the time he kept pulling away, edging toward the door, nodding and saying *"Ja, ja."* He finally got out and got the door closed, and I relaxed and hoped for the best. The sight of that food had been a jolt. A chunk of bread and a stinking dead fish! I had read of such things, but it wasn't real until I saw it there before me.

I knew I was a prisoner, and had had several days to get used to the idea. But now I began to really understand. It is one thing to say to oneself, "I am no longer a free agent, I am captive," but quite another to bump into the restraints that make for captivity, to feel the walls, to test the door, to call out a need and have it ignored. Full realization came when, as the weak light faded into blackness and the damp chill of night seeped through my clothing, I knew at last that my little jailer was not coming back with the things I had demanded.

It was during this first evening that the resolve began to form in my mind that I must escape at the first opportunity—escape with some hope of success, but escape. I hadn't gotten to the point of feeling that I would rather be dead than imprisoned; it takes a lot to push a healthy young man to that point, and I had not yet even been bruised. But that night, for the first time since my captivity, the feeling began to grow in me that I must free myself.

However, I was alive and in good condition, and although I was cold and depressed, I still had a margin of interest in my surroundings. Shortly after the guard disappeared with his bucket and tins, I became aware of the occupants of the other three cells, the two on my left as I faced the door and the one on my right. I heard talking in the cells on the left and could not identify the language.

There was talking, then some gentle calling to which a voice in the cell on my right responded. They conversed briefly, then the guy in "left," up on his bench, was trying to pass something to the guy in "right" by means of a stick made of two long slivers of wood tied together. This was possible because the wire screening above the board walls was wide mesh stuff, like very heavy chicken wire. When I saw that the stick would not reach, I plucked off the little packet and handed it to "right." The packet was wrapped with newspaper tied with string, an inch thick and two or three inches long. There was some more talk, and the guy on my left knocked on my wall and handed me a similar packet. I opened it carefully in the dim light and saw it was coarse, shredded tobacco. With it there was one match.

This gesture of fellowship cheered me up immediately. My remaining cigarettes had been taken from me on my last search, since prisoners were forbidden to smoke. Actually, the lack of tobacco had not especially bothered me, but having the makings in hand prompted me to go ahead and light up. It was floor-sweeping tobacco and, being dry, was hard to roll, but soon I was contributing to the local smudge.

These fellows were talking in a language I did not recognize or understand, but I decided to try French on the one to my left. I attracted his attention and asked, *"Parlez-vous français?"* That brought on a flow of something that sounded vaguely German.

So I tried *"Ich bin Amerikaner"* and got approving sounds this time from all three, and responses of *"Wir Rusky!"* Russians! So my cell mates, in that grim old dungeon in Lille, France, were Russians, or so they claimed. It seemed a bit odd to me, but we couldn't communicate, so I could learn no more. They were company, anyway, and inclined to be friendly.

The incident of the tobacco started me on a gloomy line of thought about how ill-equipped I was to cope with this new life. I was not only unprepared mentally for the brutal fact of imprisonment, I didn't even have the faintest notion of how to go about the business of providing myself with other than what might be given to me. By contrast, this Rusky managed to provide himself with tobacco of sorts, and matches, both forbidden to prisoners. Also, he had some sort of cutting tool that had enabled him to cut from his bench the long slivers of wood he had used in his try at passing the tobacco to the far man. I saw before me the weary prospect of learning an infinite variety of tricks to furnish myself with even the meanest comforts through the coming days, weeks, months.

As the evening wore on, and while I was pacing up and down to keep warm while thinking my gloomy thoughts, my cell mates took to singing, sometimes one man at a time, sometimes the two or three together. I didn't recognize any of the melodies, nor could I understand the words, but the effect was pleasantly distracting. In a lull, I gave voice myself with "Swanee River," "Old Black Joe," and "On the Banks of the Wabash," and through the evening I sang just about every song I knew the words to. I didn't have much of a voice, but the acoustics of that vaulted tomb persuaded me that I was doing passing well. I became so engrossed with the singing that several hours passed quite tolerably.

There was still, however, the experience of sleeping on that bench, with that tiny blanket. It was impossible to be comfortable, since the bench was designed to frustrate sleep. Then there was the experimenting with the midget blanket. I tried using it as a mat, to protect me from the floor's cold, but then I got no protection on top. On top of me the blanket would cover either the upper two-thirds or the lower two-thirds of my body, leaving one-third and the entire underside exposed.

A dozen times I got down off the bench with a curse and resumed my pacing and stamping to get warm again. Somewhere in the course of my twisting, thumping, and cursing, I went off to sleep, and was awakened in the wan light of morning by the guard bringing me my slop.

The would-be coffee I kept, since it was hot, but into the pail went the rest of the mess. Again I gave the wart of a guard the word, and this time, after a night on that slatted torture rack, there must have been a ring of earnest conviction in my voice. From then on this miserable character addressed me with some respect as *"Herr Oberleutnant,"*— but that was the only improvement.

Sometime during the morning, which I passed away doing calisthenics and lying on my bench, I became aware of an unusual racket in the little courtyard. I listened for a while, but couldn't make sense of what I heard. There was an occasional shout, like a command, but the pervading sound was a rustling shuffle of movement. But no voices other than the occasional shout.

With some effort I got myself up to where I could look over my board wall, through the screen and the narrow window across the aisle and so into the courtyard. The yard was half in sunlight, and what I saw there turned my blood cold. A single file of human beings spaced closely together, evidently extending clear around the small area, shuffled along at an even pace. No voices, only the dead shuffle of soft-soled shoes on the pavement. All the heads I saw were shaved, showing sickly gray even in the sunlight.

They shambled, vacant eyes straight ahead or cast down, men of no nationality, incomprehensible beings in nondescript clothing. I must have watched two dozen of these creatures pass my windows, not ten yards away, and they all looked alike. At a command they altered their listless walk into a macabre semblance of a trot.

I watched with a kind of horrid fascination, seeing for the first time what happened to people who for one reason or another displeased Hitler's government. I watched until I couldn't hold myself in that strained position any longer, then sat on my bench and, shaken to the depths of my soul, thought about what I'd seen.

I had read that Hitler's people handled their opponents like cattle, debased and tortured them, broke them into nonmen, but now I'd seen it—or thought I'd seen it. I realized that those prisoners were actually fairly well off: They weren't especially emaciated, and were not only given an exercise period but were able to walk and trot. Others, somewhere, must be even worse off.

What I saw was what I immediately imagined I myself would become, in time, as a prisoner. I too would have my head shaved, would be herded like an animal, would become a shambling, vacant-eyed robot, one of the living dead. The thought took out of me what little bluster and defiance I had left.

In that hour my resolve to escape hardened into a determination, a determination that from then on never left me. I knew I would either escape or be shot in the attempt. I'd seen at last something I would risk death to avoid.

The rest of the day I passed pacing, swinging my arms about, and brooding. Sometime during the afternoon the guard came in with the second, and last, meal of the day: coffee, the large chunk of bread, the dead fish staring up at me. The guard addressed me respectfully and left. This time I didn't throw the food out. Instead, with a humility I had never before felt, I got down on my knees and asked a blessing on that food, that I would be given the strength I was finally aware I could not find in myself alone. My prayer didn't improve the taste of the food, but my outlook did improve somewhat when I finally got the stuff down.

After dark I made another cigarette out of the remnants of the tobacco, got a light from the magician on my left, and we settled down for another melancholy serenade. That second night, during my pacings and in between my efforts at sleeping on the bench, my mind went continually back to the idea of escape. I was no longer willing to accept my fate. I would get away from this horror somehow.

7

Dawn of the second day came into the cell cold and gray as before, filtered through a shroud. There were no sounds except those made by my pacing and other exertions as I worked the stiffness out of my body. The feeding seemed earlier than on the previous day. The *Herrenvolk* gaoler brought coffee and bread and shuffled away, but on this second morning he was back in half an hour, beckoning me to follow him. He led me through the catacombs to the room where I had first come to know this place, but this time I didn't have long to wait. A tall soldier, a Prussian prototype in a horsehide military greatcoat, motioned me to fall in behind him and led me outside.

It was around half-past seven on a magnificent spring day. Clear air and sunshine and my sense of release magnified the beauty of the morning a thousandfold, and I pushed the picture of my cell to the back of my mind. But that picture of gray despair remained never more than a thought away. It was May 7, 1944, another day I have good reason to remember. On the sidewalk outside the prison building surrounded by a litter of suitcases and bundles stood another soldier watching the Prussian and me emerge. Short and pudgy, he was dressed in woolens and a field cap, and he peered through thick, steel-rimmed glasses.

The two talked briefly, the big, square-rigged sergeant

and the little private. Then they gathered up suitcases and packages and pointed to a bundle that apparently I was to carry. I was about to refuse when I realized that it contained my own possessions. Off we went, the Sam Goldwyn Kraut, the company clerk, and I, who must have been a sorry-looking specimen indeed. I had neither shaved nor washed properly for four days, and I had been sleeping in my uniform since my bail-out.

A short walk brought us to a railroad station, and in a few minutes we were installed in a compartment in the center of a clean, new-looking coach. The door, sliding on tracks to open and close, was glass-paneled and was kept closed while the train was in motion. The two German soldiers stowed their gear on the baggage racks and settled themselves. The big one took the seat near the window, and his companion sat beside him, next to the door to the aisle. I sat alone on the bench facing them, with the window on my left.

Immediately I began to size up escape possibilities. I assumed that I would be taken to Dulag Luft, in Frankfurt, the central interrogation center for captured airmen, but I had no idea how far it was from here to there. I knew, however, that my best chance for a getaway would be while we were still in French or Belgian territory, where I assumed I could count on help from the natives. Our escape and evasion briefings had stressed the many opportunities for escape in the course of a train trip, especially in "friendly" territory.

The compartment was roomy, and by the grace of God, or by mortal design, we were alone in it. I learned shortly, however, that this was a troop train of some twelve cars, so instead of just two enemy soldiers for escort, I had about five hundred. I also learned soon after the train got underway that there was a rest room in our car, at the end that my seat faced, and it was one of the first things I scouted. It gave me reason to be frequently at the end of the car near the exit door, and its fair-sized window presented a possible escape hatch.

As we waited for the train to pull out of Lille, I began the first stage of my escape plan: gaining the confidence of my guards. Several things were in my favor. I was small, and my unkempt condition must have made me look even more harmless to the Germans than I was; and the Hoosier friendliness I studiously applied made me appear more agreeable than I felt. These two fellows, little acquainted with one another and separated by a significant difference in rank, seemed well suited to my purposes.

My campaign was simple. I interested myself in German, in Germany, and in my guards personally. But for the first couple of hours neither of the men showed any but the most perfunctory interest in my overtures. On my first trip to the rest room, minutes after we got under way, the big one stayed with me and ordered me to leave the door open. He was armed and kept close behind me, alert the whole time.

My first real contact was made through the pictures of my wife and family. They inquired if I had any children—"*Kinder?*"—and asked where my wedding ring was. Conversation was extremely difficult. I knew only a little pillow German, which I'd picked up from my German refugee girlfriend in college, and my traveling companions had no English and precious little French, but we managed.

After my pictures had been respectfully examined, first the big man and then the other produced snapshots of wife and children. They told me their own names, and explained that they both were going home on leave. This ritual of bringing the families into view removed the chill that had emanated from both men, but I sensed they felt some reservations because I had no children to declare.

I have no idea what brought the subject up, and still less how the little man finally got across to me what he was talking about, but the pleasure all three of us found in recalling the Walt Disney movie *Snow White and the Seven Dwarfs* finally broke the ice. It was quite a scene in that coach as we regaled each other with our favorite sequences from the movie from a lost, peaceful world.

By some time before noon we were almost bosom buddies, tied by a bond of a shared experience. As if to seal a compact, the big sergeant gave me a cigarette and lighted one himself. In so doing he broke two regulations. A sign above his head said *Nicht Rauchen*, "No Smoking"; and it was forbidden to give cigarettes to prisoners in any event. When I pointed to the sign and smiled, he blew a cloud of smoke at it and pretended he couldn't read it. From that time on into the night, my new friend, Hans, shared his cigarettes with me. Although the little fellow, whose name did not stay with me, had brought up the Snow White business, he never really warmed up. He seemed pre-occupied, and left Hans and me pretty much alone.

As our conversation ranged over just about everything except the war, I tried to give it direction in order to learn some of the things I needed to know. I asked about Germany: Was it nice? Would we go to Berlin? Were the German women better than the French women? Would I be put in a prison camp in a nice part of Germany? This line gave me a chance to show a genuine interest in Germany. My key questions that followed aroused no apparent suspicion: I asked how far it was to Germany, and how long it would take us to get there.

The answers were discouraging. We would be in Metz, in the French border province of Lorraine, long before dark, and by full darkness would be through Lorraine and well into Germany. Damn! I wanted darkness, and French soil, to ease my way, and being afoot in Germany among a hostile population was not my idea of the way to go.

I had learned something of our route by the simple device of asking if we would go through Paris. Hans told me that the route was Verdun, Metz, and into Saarbrücken. He also confirmed my notion that I was being taken to Frankfurt am Main.

Through the morning and early afternoon hours, I was continually exploring ways of making a break. The simplest way seemed to be to jump from the train while we were passing through one of the many tunnels along this route. Even a chance of success depended absolutely on a combination of circumstances. It was necessary that the train be going slowly enough so I would not be killed or badly injured in the jump; there had to be a double track in the tunnel; the tunnel had to be long enough to allow me time to move in the noisy darkness; and I had to be at least close to position, near an exit and on the side of the car next to the second set of tracks, so I could just disappear without being missed immediately.

But the tunnels always came on unexpectedly, and usually our speed, which I early learned to gauge by the rhythm of the wheels clicking on the rail joints, was too great. Also, when we came upon a tunnel while I was in the compartment, the second set of rails was invariably on the other side; and the same was true while I was in the toilet, opposite the main exit from the car. Since there was no electric light in the compartment, it was pitch-dark while we were in a tunnel, and my idea was that I could simply slide the window down and jump out.

Only once, shortly after lunch, did a moment seem ripe. I was in the rest room. The little soldier stood in the aisle outside the compartment door; by now, neither man accompanied me all the way. A good fifteen or twenty feet separated us. The extra rails were in the proper position, for a change, and the train had slowed on a grade to about twenty miles per hour, a safe speed. I was just coming out of the rest room when we roared into another tunnel. It took a few seconds for the situation to register, another few for me to tighten my innards and my resolve. I was about to make my move when we flashed into the sunlight, and the opportunity was past. I had to hang on to a window ledge for a moment to steady myself.

This tunnel-jump preoccupation, culminating in the abortive effort around two in the afternoon, was in the back of my mind the whole time, but outwardly I was taking quite an interest in my companions and in the goings-on about me.

Sometime during the morning, before we three had been united through Disney, my guards walked me through three carloads of staring enemy soldiers to a baggage-car kitchen. We stood there and drank hot coffee from tin cups, then pressed back to the seclusion of our compartment. After seeing how crowded the other cars were, I knew I was getting special handling. I was probably a prize catch, since I was the first American tactical reconnaissance pilot flying from England to be taken prisoner by the Germans. The 67th Group was only one of two tactical reconnaissance outfits in England, and though we had had several men killed, I was the first to be shot down over enemy territory.

The Germans were aware, of course, of the tremendous buildup of ground and air forces in England during this period, and they knew from the massing of landing craft in the south England harbors that the invasion was not far off. Indeed, in a month less one day from the date of that train ride our armadas would smash against Hitler's Fortress Europe, sounding the crack of doom to his dream of a thousand-year Reich. The Luftwaffe would naturally be happy to hold at last a reconnaissance pilot from the air unit that had harried the coastal areas of Europe for four months. Such a flier would probably have a better understanding of the imminent invasion plans than would a fighter pilot—whose primary concern was to destroy enemy fighters and to strafe enemy ground troops—or a bomber pilot.

After the coffee break, curious soldiers began stopping in to chat with my guards and to stare at me. One visitor was a pale and bulgy *Mädchen* in uniform, who remained, flirting with my guards, for a quarter of an hour before she left us in peace. A more disquieting visitor wore the black uniform of the SS. As he stared silently from the doorway, all the evil things I had heard of Hitler's elite corps of fanatics and sadists went through my mind. Within a few minutes, much to my relief, he left. During the afternoon Sergeant Hans abruptly ordered all the sightseers away and we were bothered no more.

Lunch was quite an affair. In the midst of a lesson on how to count in German, Hans announced that it was time to eat. He hauled his tin suitcase down off the rack, took out three loaves of brown bread, a package of lard, and a large chunk of bologna. He placed them on a little folding table hinged to the wall under the window. He then took a large folding knife from his pocket and cut slabs of bread, spread them with lard, and began devouring them with chunks of the bologna. It was something to see this giant eat.

He pushed the bread and knife toward me, and when I learned that the stuff I'd thought was lard was actually an uncolored margarine, I ate with a good appetite. Hans finished two and a half loaves of bread by the time I'd eaten half of one—which, with margarine and bologna, was enough for me. That meal, shared with my new comrades, was the first I enjoyed since my capture.

Shortly after we finished, I asked the little soldier to let me examine his pistol. Both men had removed their pistols and their greatcoats, which had grown uncomfortably warm. The soldier's belted holster hung on a peg above his head and out of the way. He looked startled at my request, but at a word from Hans he slipped the weapon from its holster, snapped out the ammunition clip, and handed the gun to me. It was a formidable weapon, as clumsy in the hand as our own .45 automatic. I worked the charging mechanism, aimed carefully out the window, and squeezed the trigger. To avoid suspicion I soon handed it back, and declared that it was a much better pistol than the Americans had.

It had occurred to me during the morning to grab one of the pistols, hold the guards at bay until we reached a tunnel, where the roar would muffle the necessary shots, then simply walk down the car and jump off. When I asked to see the weapon, I wanted to learn whether they kept a shell in the chamber, and to check the charging mechanism and safety catch. But while I held the pistol with this plan in mind, I knew I could never bring myself to carry out a cold-blooded killing. Strafing cars and people from a plane at three hundred miles an hour is cool, clean, and impersonal, at least to the killer. But it is quite another thing for that same person to do cold murder at close range.

It was in the midafternoon, about an hour after my near attempt to jump in the tunnel, when my first real break came. The train stopped in a town called Charleville, close to the French-Belgian border; but instead of observing the usual pause, the train stood on a siding for nearly four hours. At first I was annoyed at the delay, a traveler's instinctive reaction, but as the time wore on, my spirits began to rise. Every hour spent standing in Charleville gave me an additional hour of darkness on French soil. The delay guaranteed that we would not cross from Lorraine into Germany before midnight.

After an hour or so of waiting, Hans became restless and went to the front of the train to see what was up. He came back cursing the ineptness of the French engineers who were repairing the broken-down engine. He explained to me, with the help of his hands, that the engine had been shot up by an American P-47 fighter (a "Jabo," he called it) a month or so before and had not been well repaired.

I joined big Hans in disparaging remarks about the French, because my pose was eagerness to see Germany by daylight. But I sent up a secret prayer of thanks to the unknown American fighter pilot who had banked his lethal weapon out of the sky and had raked the vitals of this railroad engine with his eight .50 caliber guns. That lad had brought me four precious hours in friendly territory.

We spent the afternoon in Charleville talking and gazing out the window at the busy station platform. Occasionally one of my guards would leave the compartment to walk up and down the platform or to check the progress of the engine repairs. These soldiers were going home on leave and were naturally impatient at the delay, but it became increasingly difficult for me to conceal my pleasure.

I found some diversion for a while in watching the actions of a young German pilot officer in class A uniform as he paced the platform. I had never seen, outside the movies, a smarter, more self-possessed figure than the one that fellow cut. His uniform was tailored to perfection of beautiful material, and from the top of his high-peaked officer's cap to the tip of his leather boots, he epitomized authority and arrogant self-confidence.

The sight of this young officer strengthened my disquieting suspicion that these damn fool Germans did not know they were losing the war. Not only that, from the things I had seen, I was becoming less and less sure that we had been actually beating these people down to the extent we'd been told we were. Of course I still hadn't the slightest doubt that the Allies would win eventually. I had witnessed the monumental buildup of planes and troops in the south of England these past months and knew we had overwhelming power. Besides, it was still inconceivable for an American to think in terms of losing a war. But any notion I had entertained that the invasion and the drive to Berlin would be a piece of cake was fast dissolving in the light of what I was seeing.

During the afternoon, Hans scanned the sky through the compartment window and then remarked, quite matter-of-factly, that this was *"Maraudah vetteh."* I caught it and grinned, knowing that the 9th Air Force B-26s, the Martin Marauders, bombed targets in France—mainly the robot-bomb sites—only in clear weather. My understanding was that they required one-tenth or less cloud cover for their strikes, since their targets were extremely difficult to spot and they bombed from medium heights at high speed. So to this soldier, and to others like him who manned the guns around the "ski sites," a lovely clear day was *"Maraudah vetteh!"*

8

At last the engine was repaired, and signals were made to get all the passengers aboard. When we got under way again, it must have been close to seven o'clock, since we'd had another meal of bread, margarine, and, this time, cheese, while still halted in Charleville. This promised to be a beautiful, clear night, and my chest was tight with expectancy. As dusk and then darkness gathered, we passed the time away singing, and I concentrated on lullabies. I joined with Hans in a little harmony on Brahms's "Lullaby" and gave a soulful rendition of "Old Black Joe." Even the private joined in on some of the singing, and our day of brotherhood eased into a somnolent night.

By evening I was able to tell to my complete satisfaction when the train was traveling slowly enough for a safe jump. I had thought so much about it that regardless of what I was doing or thinking at a given moment, I was automatically aware when the clicking rhythm of the wheels indicated a slowdown to a safe speed. My guess was that twenty-five miles per hour was the top of the safe range.

A couple of times that evening, in order to have an idea of how much time I had to work with, I asked how far it was to Metz. Hans gave me the distance in kilometers, and after mentally converting to miles and dividing our estimated average speed of forty-five miles per hour into the total, I came out with a 2 A.M. arrival time in Metz. Less than half an hour after going through Metz we would cross the border into Germany, so I figured that before two in the morning I had to be off that train and long gone if I was to make my getaway in friendly territory.

I'm surprised that my repeated checking of the time with the little soldier, coupled with what I felt was my all-too-obvious restlessness, didn't make my guards suspicious. But after we had sung for a while in the darkness, the pair set about making themselves comfortable for the night.

Our positions in the compartment hadn't changed. The two Germans were on the one bench, Hans nearest the window, and I had the other bench entirely to myself. Both men had put their greatcoats back on, and although Hans left his pistol and belt, rolled together, overhead on the baggage rack, the other fastened his gunbelt around his waist and settled back in his corner. I did the best I could to make my unpadded bones comfortable on the hard upholstery and shivered in the cold of the unheated compartment.

Even though there was no light in our compartment, a brilliant moon reflected off the landscape to provide enough light inside so that I could see well enough. Occasionally, as we wound our twisted way along, our side of the train came broadside of the moon and the compartment was brightly lighted. The feeling grew within me that soon now I would get my chance. Everything was right: It was night, we would be in France for some hours yet, and my guards trusted me. The fact that we three were alone in the compartment gave me my greatest advantage.

Faced with a dangerous decision, I was troubled by conflicting impulses. I had a very strong urge to stay put, to court no danger, to rock along in certain safety with these two trusting fellow soldiers. Besides, these fellows, Hans particularly, had been very decent to me, and I felt some responsibility toward them. My escaping would undoubtedly get these men—husbands and fathers both of them—into serious trouble.

But stronger than this wish to be safe and kind was the remembrance of the prison in Lille and what I had seen there. The awful possibility, however remote, of becoming like one of those zombies in the courtyard was intolerable. I could not let that happen if I could avoid it.

With my guards apparently settling down for some rest, my excitement grew. I lay down in order to seem at least to be trying to sleep, but the cold and my tenseness soon forced me upright and occasionally set my hands to shaking. Once, as I was pretending sleep, I heard the train begin to slow down, and with heart pounding, I quietly brought myself to my feet. The train was going around a bend, and as the shaft of moonlight reached the little man's face, I saw that his eyes were wide open, regarding me. I muttered that I was cold, and began working my shoulders and rubbing my hands, and then sat down again and stared out the window.

After the train had picked up speed, I thought I might test the soldier's confidence in me and try to encourage it. I had only this little one to worry about now, since Hans had settled into snoring slumber, leaving the private to stand watch. I stood up, stretched, flexed my knees, and stepped to the door, muttering "latrine" to explain where I was going.

Train noises drowned the small sound made by the door as I opened it; I shut it carefully behind me and walked down the aisle to the rest room. Once around the corner, I peered cautiously back and saw that my guard had not followed me out into the aisle. I headed back presently to the compartment but stood a few moments in the aisle outside, working the stiffness from my legs and arms; I knew that would look all right to the private. Since I had no overcoat, he must have realized that I was cold and needed to exercise to get warm.

When I reentered the compartment and sat down, I asked my guard what time it was. He showed me his watch, and the luminous dial told me it was some minutes past eleven. I pushed myself into the corner of my seat nearest the door, put my feet up on the seat, and tried to relax. Sometime later, the German seemed to find his pistol belt uncomfortable: He took it off and laid the weapon—holster flap up, gun butt outward—on the seat between him and Hans. He then leaned forward, elbows on knees and face cupped in his hands. He shifted his position a few times; finally he seemed to be asleep.

As I sat there, I dozed off and on, although the numbing cold made me shiver violently at times. But I snapped wide awake out of my shallow sleep as the clicking wheels signaled a slowing down. Neither man opposite me stirred, and I knew that this was the chance I must grasp.

In those few passing moments as the train slowed toward safe speed, I got into gear, clear in my mind and uncommonly steady. I swung feet to floor cautiously, and once standing, held still for a moment. Neither of the Germans moved. When my eye caught the gleam of the holster on the seat between them, I obeyed an insane impulse. I stooped over, stole the pistol naked from its holster, and stuck it in my waistband as I slid the door open with my left hand. I dreaded that the cold current of the air from the aisle would wake the enemy, but they remained still. I eased the door shut behind me and started down the aisle, pulling my jacket over the butt of the gun.

The exit door was twenty feet away—agonizingly distant. My back, turned toward danger, began to ache with anticipation of the blow I was sure would come. As I walked, a new fear seized me: I would be seen by one of the hundreds of other enemy soldiers crowding this train, since the rest room I must pass served the two adjacent cars as well as our own.

When I reached the open door of the car, I looked back. There was no sign of disturbance. I stepped down to the bottom mounting step, and holding the hand rail with my right hand, hung crouched down, facing the front of the train. The sharp, cold wind exhilarated me as I timed myself to jump between the telegraph poles that flashed by in the silvery night. I picked my space, and at the right moment let go and was tumbled roughly, head-over-heels, in the gravel of the roadbed.

I lay still, head down, until the last car had bustled past, then raised my head to watch it disappear into the night. I listened anxiously for a hullabaloo, the screech of emergency brakes announcing that I had been missed, but the diminishing sound of the train quickly pulsed into silence. I was free! I started running away from the tracks, laboring over newly plowed ground, as fast as I could go.

9

I galloped through the moonlit night over sod and plowed ground for a quarter of a mile, then flung myself down on my back to rest and take stock. There was a cathedral stillness in the world, and the stars were pale and soft in the presence of the stark silver of the moon. The freshly turned earth had a smell that I knew and loved, and as I lay there, my breath regained, I felt clean and at peace with the night and with myself. By an act of will, I had broken free and altered my destiny. This realization restored the self-confidence I was not fully-aware I had lost.

There was still the problem of getting out of France, which was for all practical purposes enemy country. That meant heading for neutral Spain, because I knew that from there I could get back to England. Spain was five hundred miles to the south as the crow flies, but I had no idea how I was to get there. I would need food and shelter, acceptable clothing in place of my uniform, guidance past the Germans. But I would worry about that later. For the present I would simply start walking southward. I searched the wan stars and located the Big Dipper, and from it the North Star, the only compass left me.

The North Star told me I had been running north instead of south, so I got up, retraced my steps at a walk, and went across the rails in the other direction. A hundred yards or so past the tracks ran a country road, just beyond which was a canal or small river about fifteen yards wide.

That stopped me. Just visible to my left was a stone bridge across the water, but I guessed it would be guarded. To my right, about a quarter of a mile down the road, there was a cluster of houses, and I could hear music, laughter, and chatter. Remembering strict advice against approaching crowds of people, even Frenchmen, I decided that my best course was to get away in the other direction, even though it was north.

In spite of my fear of the railroad, which I had been warned would likely be patrolled regularly, I again started back toward it, but paused by a clump of small trees to force myself to think calmly about what I must do. As I stood there, I noticed that the music had stopped and, from the shouting and calling, guessed that the party or dance was breaking up. This suggested two things to me: It was probably around midnight; and if some of these people passed by me, I could listen to their talk and know whether I was in France or Germany.

So I hid in that clump of trees beside the road and listened to the approach of two men from the party. As they passed I made out that they were talking French, and from then on I acted on the assumption that I was in France.

When the two men were out of hearing I began walking. I recrossed the tracks and walked over wide, rolling fields, sometimes feeling cultivated ground underfoot and sometimes sod. The German pistol was a galling weight that pulled at my waistband and kept recalling a vague worry that nagged at me from the back of my mind.

I noticed the frequent occurrence of high hedges that seemed to project haphazardly out into the fields, ending abruptly. I decided to push my way through one such hedge instead of walking around its end—and saved myself from falling into a deep hole only by grabbing the bush beside me. I sat there on the edge of that hole for a bit, puzzled. And suddenly it came to me: These must be

World War I trenches that, instead of being filled in, had been allowed to grow over with brush.

In saving myself from falling, I had twisted around and landed on my stomach on the edge of the trench, ramming the heavy pistol into my abdomen. It nearly knocked the wind out of me, and I began thinking soberly about the weapon. Like most men in my squadron, I never carried a pistol on my combat missions. I assumed that, should a man be shot down and brought to bay, the Germans would be less likely to shoot an unarmed man than an armed one. That reasoning had force in my present situation, and since I couldn't picture myself waving that hand cannon at anyone anyway, I pitched it into the trench and was relieved to be rid of it.

On I went, keeping clear of those grim relics of another war, which showed black in the night's bright light. Once I came upon a cemetery, and thinking it would be an ideal place to hide through the coming day, I climbed the fence to have a look around.

It was situated on the crown of a little hill, spilling over each slope, and would be a fine vantage point from which to survey a route by daylight. As I worked my way toward the center, however, I saw something that froze me in my tracks: Silhouetted against the sky was something that looked very much like the barrel of an antiaircraft gun. I crouched down and listened for a long time, more and more certain that it *was* a cannon I saw there. Satisfied finally that I had not been seen nor heard, I carefully retraced my steps out of that place.

With my fears again aroused, that impression of Germans being all over the face of this country returned. And again my imagination began to play tricks on me: What had previously passed as bushes and trench hedges began to look more like trucks, tents, and hutments. But I had to push on, and did—taking, it seemed to me, fearful chances.

At last I became aware that the moonlight had thinned and that the shadows were graying ever so slightly—daybreak was coming. I had to find a place to hide. Down a slope, to my left and half a mile away, was a small cluster of buildings, and beyond it, halfway to a long winding strip of undergrowth in a shallow valley, stood a large strawstack. A wagon track came from the house, running past the strawstack, through the underbrush strip, and into the wide fields rising beyond.

In the first light of early morning, I reached the strawstack, climbed up it, and covered myself over. Although I couldn't get warm, I finally did doze off, and woke to find the sun up and the chill gradually leaving my body.

I raised myself from my musty hole to see what the world looked like by daylight. The wagon track led up a gentle slope to what I could now see were farm buildings, and beyond them to a small village, which I had not noticed the night before because of its many trees. To my left the wagon road led down to a line of trees and brush at the bottom of a valley, where there was evidently a creek. The fields beyond were dreary and tired-looking in the early morning light.

I saw the roof of a small house where the wagon track crossed the wooded strip, and decided to investigate it. The strawstack was out in the open, giving me no real cover unless I stayed in it, and I had no stomach for a day in that moldy, bug-ridden heap.

The little house actually straddled the creek. It had been some sort of a springhouse but was in disrepair and showed no signs of recent use. It gave me an ideal vantage point, because from its door I could see both ways up the wagon road. The part of the roof that was intact would give me shade from the sun, and at long last I could do some kind of a job washing myself in the creek.

After I'd washed, I found a concealed spot in back of the hut, stretched out in the warm morning sunlight, and soon fell asleep. The sound of a wagon coming down the way awakened me, and I peered out to see a youngish man driving a one-horse cart down toward the fields. Seeing no one else about, I decided to stop him and ask for food.

Our escape and evasion briefings had cautioned us to

approach only lone individuals, and always as far as possible from habitations and from other people. Under such circumstances, if the native should prove hostile or unsympathetic, the evader would still have a chance to make himself scarce before the other fellow could give him too much trouble. Also, a man who might, on his own, be inclined to extend aid could very well be afraid of being informed upon if approached in the presence of others.

My spot was ideal for my purposes, out of sight of the buildings and leaving me good concealment should a retreat become necessary. As the man approached the creek, I stepped out the door of the springhouse and hailed him, smiling and showing empty hands.

I gave him my *bonjour* and explained in my best Manchester College French that I was an American pilot, that I had recently parachuted into France. I didn't tell him I had just escaped from the Germans, since I thought that the bounty might be a little higher for an escaped prisoner. I told him I was hungry and thirsty and asked, *"Voulez-vous m'aider?"* "Will you help me?"

The man was about thirty, I guessed, but his face and body gave the impression that he worked hard and was worn beyond his years. He seemed interested in what I said, if a little bemused at the intrusion of the war into his routine of toil. He directed me to wait, then went off with his wagon toward the fields. I kept my eyes on him, because he now had knowledge that could do me great harm.

He drove well into the nearest field, unloaded a harrow from the wagon, and then came directly back. He got down from the wagon, beckoned to me, and together we walked toward the buildings, he leading his horse. We went directly to one of the buildings, a quaint little stone house surrounded by a yard of packed dirt, and he led me into a kitchen that stank of garbage and many generations of sour milk. My friend spoke to his wife, a plump young woman with a pimply face, and she set a mug of milk on the table before me. I thanked her and forced myself to drink it all, though getting anything down amid that stench was an ordeal. I felt guilty at my revulsion, because I was aware that in giving me food and shelter these kind people were risking their lives. As I drank, both the man and the woman watched me with wonder, as though they were seeing a creature from another world.

I could not understand much of their talk, and could only imagine that they understood me, so there was not much conversation. Feeling the need to persuade them that I was genuine, I gave my family pictures another airing. My hosts seemed to be very much interested, especially when I explained that my father was a farmer, *"comme vous,"* "like you."

When I got the idea across that I wanted a place to hide during the day, the man took me out to the barn and showed me the way to the haymow. The sides of the building were board, so set that wide cracks were left between them. My hideout gave me plenty of fresh air and enabled me to watch the goings-on around the house and around the village, a couple hundred yards beyond. I watched from this place to see what the man would do, and was reassured when, after a short stop at the house, he retraced his way to the fields.

I dozed through the morning, and was awakened by the man at noon to drink the milk and eat the bread and hard sausage he had brought. Toward the evening, with the sun low and the air beginning to chill, the man returned with another cup of milk, two small loaves of dark bread, and a supply of assorted bolognas. The bread and meat were provisions for my travel, which, he conveyed pointedly, should begin as soon as darkness fell. He also gave me a little packet of tobacco, some cigarette papers, and several large, crude matches. I thanked him as well as I could, and that was the last I saw of him.

Only the faded remnants of a beautiful sunset remained when I left the barn, my jacket bulging with the provisions. I felt a bit ungainly carrying the stuff, but it was food and not to be left behind. I had decided during the day that I would travel north and west most of the night, then bear to the south and try to negotiate, in the first light of early morning, the canal that had daunted me the night before. So off I went, feeling rested and full of confidence.

10

When I had gone a couple of miles, I stopped and after some difficulty with the coarse, stringy tobacco, constructed a cigarette of sorts. This cigarette, this lumpy thing with shreds sprouting obscenely out of both ends, started a chain of events that determined the course of my entire escapade. I have often wondered how things would have worked out if that farmer had simply omitted the tobacco, or at least the matches, from the supplies he gave me.

Those matches, somewhat resembling kitchen matches I was familiar with, were larger and had bulbous heads. When struck, instead of flaring to a yellow flame and igniting the wood, this first French match sputtered with a small, uncertain flame.

Since I was expecting a flare, I left the flame unprotected, and a breeze blew it out before I could light up. So on the second match I cupped the sputtering flame and put it to my cigarette instantly. What I got instead of a light was a strong, nasty lungful of sulphur fume that nearly knocked my head off. The trick, I learned later, was to let the initial sulphur flame ignite the larger head, which would in turn fire the matchstick.

With my throat burning and the acrid taste of sulphur in my mouth, I walked on, developing a thirst that grew more and more demanding. After an hour I felt I could drink

anything liquid, and when I saw the church spire of a
village ahead of me and to the right, I made up my mind to
go and ask at some house for a drink, and to hell with the
risk.

I pushed on into the village, a fair-sized one that I later
learned was called Boinville. A careful reconnaissance
showed me nobody was stirring in the streets, but I thought
it better to approach a back door anyway. It was puzzling
to fumble around in the dark through the backyards of that
village until I realized that barns and houses here were all
one. I had heard of the intimacy with which French farmers
shared accommodations with their stock, but the farm I
had stayed at during the day had not been like these; its
barns were some distance from the house. Besides, I didn't
expect to find farmers in the village.

I bumbled through several barnyards looking for a house-
barn where a light showed. I found a couple, but my
knocking at the back doors and windows brought no response except the dousing of the lights. It occurred to me
that I might do better at a house somewhat detached from
the village, so that I could call out with some safety.

I followed along parallel with a street, and went onto the
road as soon as it left the houses. It made a turn and
shortly crossed some railroad tracks (my railroad, I thought).
I stepped boldly across the tracks and continued on down
the road a ways to an isolated group of buildings. I could
hear voices in the house and decided I should go around to
the back, where I could get closer and listen with less
chance of being spotted. My thirst was by now a frantic
thing.

Instinct urged caution, because I could hear several voices
in the house, but my epic thirst urged me on. The house
was built on a slope down from the road, and I found a
door that led into a ground-level cellar lighted by a single
dim bulb, under the main part of the house. The cellar
smelled strongly of milk and cheese. A plain plank stairway
ascended into shadow to the first floor. Now I heard the
upstairs voices much more distinctly. They were speaking
French, and I could pick out two female voices and one

male. A fourth voice was that of either a young boy or a girl. I looked for a water faucet but found none, so I decided to approach the owners of the voices I heard.

As I stood in the dim light of the cellar, I tried to evaluate the risk I was taking in approaching these people. That they were speaking French weighed more heavily with me than it should have. At the time, I'd talked myself into assuming that all French people were willing to risk their lives in opposition to the Germans. I suspected, though, that some kind of reward—one that in these straitened times might be a real incentive—awaited the citizen who would turn an Allied airman over to the Germans. It also occurred to me that my absence from the train might have been noticed in time so that my general whereabouts was known and I would be too "hot" to be sheltered.

On the other hand, this house stood some distance from the village, with open country all around, and the darkness would help my getaway if I had reckoned wrong.

Just as I started for the stairs I heard the quick click of a woman's heels overhead, and abruptly the door to the cellar stairway opened. I backed into shadow and watched a beautiful pair of legs wade gingerly down into the dim light; legs, then shapely hips in a tight skirt, and finally the entire Junoesque figure of a young woman. She was of medium height, with thick black hair, and her face was handsome.

Preoccupied with not tripping on the rough steps, she reached the bottom step, and I moved into the light, stopped, and addressed a greeting in my pleasantest French. From the look of startled fear on her face, one might have thought Himmler himself stood there before her. She began speaking French in gasps as she backed up the steps: "What do you want? Go away! Who are you? Go away!"

I spoke soothingly, made no move to go closer to her, and asked her to wait.

"*Un moment, s'il vous plait. Je suis américain.*" All I wanted, I said, was some water. "*J'ai soif, j'ai besoin de l'eau, s'il vous plait.*" Some water, for God's sake, and I would leave.

Then she said a surprising thing. "No, you are not an American. This is a trick!" Some trick! I begged her not to go away, and to prove I was an American I undertook to get out my dog tags, which I still wore around my neck. To get at them I had to unload my rustic provisions from my jacket, and it was probably the ridiculous figure I cut, standing there in the feeble light dragging the small loaves of bread and chunks of meat from my jacket front, that took the edge off her fears.

Abruptly she beckoned me to come up the stairs, keeping some distance ahead of me and chattering at a great rate to the people in the room beyond. When I came into the room, well lighted by a simple chandelier, I saw a man seated, facing me across a round dining table; seated beside him was a towheaded lad of about twelve. My discoverer and another woman a few years older stood round-eyed behind the man.

The man looked to be in his middle forties and was on the stout side; his pleasant face was relaxed but inquiring. He didn't appear to be either hostile or suspicious. "You speak English?" he asked—in English.

Relieved, I started explaining who I was and what I wanted, but he held up his hand with a smile and said, "No speak much English." So in French I told him I was very thirsty, that I only wanted some water and I would go away.

Gesturing toward a pot and some cups on the table, he asked me if I wanted some coffee, but I declined. He then asked if I would prefer wine. "*Non, merci,*" I said. "*Seulement de l'eau, s'il vous plait.*" Water, *please*.

He spoke to the older woman, who left the room and returned soon with a pitcher of water and a glass. As they watched, I poured one glass after another and drank it greedily until the pitcher was empty. I set glass and pitcher down with a sigh of relief, thanked them, and prepared to leave.

The man spoke to the woman in French, "*Il est vraiment*

un Américain!'' Then with a laugh he said to me in halting English, ''I believe you. I have known your people in the other war, and I know that only Americans will drink water so!''

11

"I believe you!" The importance of the Frenchman's remark didn't register immediately. With my thirst quenched, I thought only that it was good that the man had no qualms about me. Then, as I stood there basking stupidly in the physical warmth of the room, it occurred to me that if this Frenchman had associated with Americans before, and if he believed my story, he might be willing to help me.

The women did not protest the man's judgment. When he asked me to sit down and join him in a cup of coffee, the older woman brought me a chair while the other one fixed my coffee. Neither concealed her nervousness, however. The man asked me how I came to be there, and I told him. The young boy, his son, listened, round-eyed.

My appearance certainly bore out my story, unshaved and unkempt as I was. The Frenchman then explained that the younger woman's obvious fear of me was based on the knowledge that German agents were known to dress in American airmen's uniforms and go about soliciting aid from French people, and anyone who lent assistance would be in for serious trouble. Considering that they were subject to such a threat, I've never ceased to marvel that these people did not turn me in straightaway. It is a nice bit of irony that my thirst for so plain a beverage as water—a thirst ignited by that sulphur match—provided the clinching evidence to the man that I was indeed an American.

This evening marked the beginning of my appreciation of simple human courage as I saw it in the French people I met. Just as my respect for the German military increased the more I saw of it, so did my wonder at the courage of the French, as I saw more and more instances of the risks they took in defiance of their conquerors. The French people who sheltered me were not simply risking a fine or a slap on the wrist; they were gambling with their lives and the lives of their families and friends. Looked at soberly, it was madness to help an Allied airman, since all they saved him from was the inconvenience and discomfort of a prison camp. For that, and for the satisfaction it gave them to defy the Germans, they risked their own destruction.

We talked for a while, and then my new friend went into a huddle with the women, who were sisters, I learned. Afterward he explained to me that I was to sleep there in that house, and early the next morning go along the highway leading to Verdun, to a spot that he would describe to me. There I was to wait, in concealment, until he came along during the morning.

He then gave me a small map of the area, taken from an almanac, showed me how to reach the rendezvous by walking across the fields, and explained that a detour around the village of Herméville was necessary because of a barricade and checkpoint along the main road. Once again I had managed to pick an area crowded with Germans. They maintained a large prison camp nearby and kept considerable troops about to guard it.

We talked a little longer, then the younger sister, the handsome one, led me to a small room upstairs and showed me the bed I was to occupy. I regret that what appears to have been an ideal setup for a romantic interlude, however brief, produced nothing, although I confess to having felt some such stray notions at the time.

My hostess, however, had completely different thoughts. She was still highly suspicious of me and scared to death of the implications of sheltering an American. The Frenchman explained later that the two sisters were Italian nationals, aliens in France, and although they owned this *fromagerie*, they did not share the hatred of the Germans that most of the people in this part of France felt. The Frenchman, who did their financial management for them, had prevailed upon the girls, against their better judgment, to shelter me for the night.

When swivel-hips had turned back my blankets and instructed me to remove only my shoes, she gave me another suspicious once-over and left. I was asleep as soon as my head hit the pillow, too sleepy to enjoy even briefly the luxury of my first real bed in five nights.

I seemed scarcely to have fallen asleep when the girl waked me, none too gently, and said it was time to go. It was still dark outside, and my first thought was that she had changed her mind and was turning me out cold. I was angry with her, and told her it was still too dark, and to call me later. But she insisted it was four-thirty and would be daylight by the time I'd had some coffee.

So I pulled on my shoes over my evil-smelling socks and clumped down to the kitchen. She showed me where I could wash, and after coffee, bread, and butter, I felt a little more civil toward this poor, scared creature. She gave me an old pair of denim trousers, a workman's jacket, and a beret for disguise, and when I was finally pulled together my uniform was completely concealed.

After eating I got out my map, oriented myself from the back door, and prepared to set out in the first light of morning. I thanked the girl with genuine gratitude, and felt that her all-too-evident relief at finally seeing the last of me was some measure of reward to her for her efforts on my behalf.

That six-mile walk on the morning of May 9 was a real pleasure. Refreshed by the sleep and the breakfast, I was able to enjoy what I have always considered the most beautiful part of the day, the hushed, clean hour before sunrise with the birds only beginning their excited twitter. The course the Frenchman had laid out for me took me about four miles west and then straight north a couple of

miles to the main highway. The pivot point for the turn
north was the little village of Herméville, which the
Frenchman had cautioned me to avoid. The prison camp
was situated a mile or so northeast of the village.

I rested for a few moments on a hill overlooking the
village and took in the sights and sounds and smells of the
just-waking countryside, and I savored the still glory of
the day's breaking as I looked upon this little out-of-the-way
French village. Smoke was beginning to rise from the
chimneys, straight and undisturbed in the quiet air, and the
mist still swathed the low places. Now that I had friends in
this land, I felt a special warmth for Herméville village, and
I projected upon it all the affection that my new position in
life had aroused in me.

Eight years later I was struck by a passage in William
Hillman's biography of President Truman's reminiscence of
his last battery fire in World War I, on the morning of
November 11, 1918. Mr. Truman states that he directed his
fire on "a little village—Hermaville—northeast of Verdun."
I was curious to learn if this was the Herméville I had
looked upon that morning of May 9, 1944, its name altered
slightly by an error of spelling or typesetting. I wrote to the
President, describing the precise location of my Herméville,
and he replied promptly that it was indeed the village he
had fired upon.

So this little French village has unwittingly featured in
important moments in the lives of at least two American
soldiers. Captain Harry S Truman fired, with considerable
relief, his last hostile rounds of World War I upon it; and
1st Lt. John F. Hickman cast upon it his blessing, relieved
to be at last among friends.

The directions had been precise, and I found my rendezvous on the highway before the sun was very high in the
sky. It was a little stone hut, a sort of way station whose
original purpose I could not figure out. Behind it, and
parallel with the road at this point, was a ridge about five
feet high. Behind the grassy ridge was a little copse of
saplings and brush, and it was there rather than in the hut
that I decided to wait for my friend. It was an ideal loafing

place, but as the sun became warmer I grew sleepy. I was afraid I might doze off and miss my man altogether, so I took up a position where I could watch the road from concealment.

It was well traveled, being the main highway between Verdun and Metz, and I was disturbed to see the rather formidable amount of military traffic that passed by. As the sun went higher and higher, I began to wonder if my friend had forsaken me, which it seemed to me would be the sensible thing for him to do. Around midmorning, however, a tandem bicycle carrying the Frenchman and the boy stopped at the hut, and I rose from my concealment.

We shook hands around, and the man explained that he and I would ride on the bicycle and the boy would hitchhike. I learned for the first time that our destination was Verdun, about eleven miles away, where my friend had his home. We wasted no time, and in short order I was pedaling second position along this French highway on the first tandem bicycle I had ever ridden. It went a bit wobbly at first, but I soon got the knack of the thing and we ate up the miles at a good, steady pace. After perhaps an hour and a half, we wheeled off the road to a wayside tavern. My friend explained that the owner was known to him and was reliable and that although most of the patrons of this bistro were trustworthy, I should say nothing, but should watch my guide's signals and do as he instructed.

So in we went, the well-dressed, stocky French businessman, and I, unshaven and tatterdemalion in my ill-fitting denims bulging over my concealed uniform. I evidently wasn't as suspicious-looking as I felt, because nothing untoward occurred—except that I got tight. I thought we would stop in and have one or two glasses of wine and then be on our way. Little did I know!

There were two men standing at the bar when we came in, and both of them shook hands with my host, and with me as well, cordially. The wine was dry and seemed to be very weak, but I enjoyed it thoroughly: Once more I was treated as a friend and not a pariah. Of course, I could not participate in the conversation, since my halting French would have given me away. As a matter of fact, I couldn't even follow the rapid-fire French, so I could not have contributed even had I been free to try.

Worse, I couldn't refuse the continued refilling of my glass, as that might have required explanations I didn't dare undertake. As time passed, more men drifted in, and I found myself alternately shaking hands with the newcomers (this was the handshakingest bunch of people I'd ever seen) and trying to dodge the ever-tilting bottle. Before long there were a dozen men in our crowd, and each newcomer had bought a round of drinks.

My friend had seemingly forgotten all about me, and as the terrible realization came to me that I was getting drunk, I worried about how I could get my friend aside and explain my problem. The wine may have been weak, but so was my resistance, since I hadn't eaten well in some time and had been under considerable strain the past several days. My ears began to ring and the floor felt oddly light beneath my feet—two signs long familiar to me—but my host was contributing to the general clatter of conversation and paying no heed at all to me.

When I finally did get the Frenchman's attention, I asked him where the rest room was, and together we went out the back door. When I had him alone I explained that I was getting drunk but was afraid to refuse the offers of wine. He agreed with my suggestion that we move on, and after a concluding round of handshaking, we started out the door. At the door we met the boy, who had only just managed a ride this far. My host explained to him that we were on our way, and we headed for the tandem.

But as soon as I stepped out into the heat of the noonday sun, I was finished. My host didn't seem to notice my unsteadiness as he readied the rig, but as I stared, dazed, about me, I saw that the lad watched us expectantly from the doorway. With a deal of puffing and a stream of expositional French from the keyman, we finally got into position for the launching: right legs over the saddles, left legs bracing us upright, the cycle aimed for the road.

The Frenchman signaled and surged forward, but I missed

the signal and felt the seat slide out from under me. I landed on the rear fender, my arms straining to hold on to the fixed rear handlebars. I tried to join in on the initial push even from this awkward position, but my frantic left foot couldn't seem to make traction in the loose gravel, and my right foot lost the other pedal and was pawing to regain it. So the Frenchman had to fight me as well as inertia and gravity in his efforts to get the contraption rolling. For a moment there seemed to be lunging legs everywhere, pistoning air and gravel as the bike slackened and veered into a tighter circle toward the inevitable fall. And fall we did, the Frenchman first, with me and the rig on top of him.

We untangled ourselves, straightened out the tandem, and stood there a few moments, my host delivering himself of a few hundred words of impassioned elaboration on his previous instructions. The only thing that got through to me, apart from the fine spray that accompanied his words, was the realization that the Frenchman was almost as drunk as I was. His oratory completed, he indicated with a flourish that we would have another try at the machine, which I am certain was also drunk. We assumed the position, and this time I got the signal, so we lunged together for Verdun.

It seemed for a moment that we were going to gain enough speed to overcome our internal imbalance, but at just the critical point my right foot slipped off the pedal. This time I tried simply to keep both feet clear and let the number-one man pump us to operating speed, but I took unaccountably to seesawing, first one foot scraping the ground and then the other, my shifting weight swinging the whole issue first this way and then that. The Frenchman put up a game fight, straining at the pedals and turning the wheel as necessary to accommodate the gyrating madness that had set in on the American half of the cycle. But one lurch pulled him a mite too far to the left, and we rammed to a halt in a hedge just short of the road.

The Frenchman knew when he was licked. After a brief rest he backed the family vehicle out of the hedge and wheeled it over to the bistro. Without a word he went back into the building, and I sat down with my back against the wall, eyes closed, to reflect upon the mechanics of motion. A few minutes later my host came back with another man and I was led to a truck, its uncovered bed loaded with milk cans. My friend's companion was the driver of the truck. He helped me to the seat beside him, and soon we were on our way, leaving the father-and-son team behind with the tandem.

12

I'm a little fuzzy about the ride into Verdun. The driver, I recall, was small, and his lean, leathery face and worn hands were those of a workingman. He listened to my tirades against the Germans, but didn't say much, probably because he couldn't make out from my brand of French what I was talking about. Eventually we stopped at a modest house on the edge of Verdun and entered a kitchen populated by a plump woman, the truck driver's wife, and his several politely curious children. My fervent talkativeness had given way by now to such a fatigue that I could scarcely keep my eyes open. We sat down at the table, and while a hubbub of chatter and activity eddied around me, I ate—and steadfastly refused any wine, which was poured from a demijohn in the center of the table.

After we had eaten, I told them I was very tired and asked if I might rest a bit. These sweet, friendly people were suddenly all abustle to see after my comfort; and so eager did they seem to do things for me I thought to ask the big favor: Could someone please wash my socks? They were so soiled by now, and so damnably uncomfortable, that I was ready to shuck them and go barefoot. The lady of the house laughed, ordered me to take my socks off, and brought me a pan of water to wash my feet in. She then

gave me a clean pair of socks to wear and carted off the
offensive ones I had been wearing. I lay down and was
soon dead to the world.

Sometime late in the afternoon, the man who had driven
me there, to his home, wakened me. He escorted me, much
refreshed, back to the kitchen, where sat my friend with
the tandem bicycle. We had a good laugh over the tavern
affair, but I took considerable pains to explain to the folks
that I had gotten drunk only because the situation had been
out of my control. These people were risking a great deal to
help me, and I did not want them to think I would wilfully
and foolishly get smashed and expose them to danger.

My friend, of the bicycle, whose name I now learned was
René Méssager, explained that I was to stay with him at his
house, some distance from this one, until arrangements
might be made to smuggle me away somewhere. I got the
idea that evening, and over the next week, that René an
accountant who did business for a number of people in
and around Verdun. The two girls of the cheese dairy were
clients of his, as was the truck driver. René was a good
man to know, since he had wide contacts and knew his way
around. In the early evening he and I took our leave, the
woman warmly promising to send my socks over the next
day. The truck driver took out his billfold and gave me a
one-hundred-franc note, explaining that a man should have
a little money with him at all times. I still have no idea
what was the real value of the franc in occupied France,
but that gift was very touching. I thanked him and we left.

We rode the tandem, this time successfully, through
several residential sections, and eventually stopped in front
of a two-story, very presentable residence. It was a two-
apartment building, the upper floor of which René and his
family occupied. There was an outside entry to the stairway,
and at the head of the stairs, which came on to a hallway,
we entered a door to the left. There, in a large kitchen-
living room, I met my host's wife, a youngish but very
tired-looking woman with a sweet face. René later told me
that she was ill, and unable to recuperate because she was

required by the Germans to work several days a week as a charwoman in official buildings. She received me very graciously, and although I had the feeling all the time I was with them that she did not like the idea of my being there, she never was anything but friendly and helpful. The lad's name was Robert. He was their only child, and for a boy of twelve he showed a most remarkable forbearance at the intrusion of an alien into his home and life.

As soon as he had introduced me to his wife, René led me to a door which, from the arrangement of the kitchen, I supposed led to a pantry. Instead it was a small bedroom with a single window looking out on the side yard. This was to be my room. I am certain, from the way it was equipped, that they had moved out of their own bedroom so I could have it.

The reason for lodging me there was soon evident. Although the Méssagers had a parlor directly across the hall from the kitchen, it was like the parlors of our grandparents in midwestern America, all fixed up but rarely used. Since the kitchen doubled as living room, again much like farm kitchens at home, this bedroom was in easy reach for me to duck into if anyone unreliable appeared unexpectedly. Several times I was hustled off into my room for three or four hours, until the coast was clear.

Once, I was required to hide under the bed, since a suspicious visitor had to be shown that there was nothing to hide. A man with highly polished black shoes, he was brought in on the pretext of inspecting a side of illegal bacon that René kept in the bedroom closet, but actually to see for himself that there was no one in that little room.

Life soon settled into a pleasant routine at 26 Avenue d'Etain, and in retrospect it seems I was there considerably longer than only eight days. Robert and I usually kept busy working in the garden, which was at the foot of a hill about half a mile away. In the evenings, after supper, René and I listened to the British Broadcasting Company French language broadcasts—a practice forbidden by the Germans under stiff penalty. Then René would lecture me at great length. He would forget that I understood little French, and none at all when delivered at 250 words a minute. About all I could do was shake my head, nod, express surprise at the apparently appropriate times, and fight to keep awake.

In many small ways, my host and his family showed their eagerness to make my stay as pleasant as possible. The meals were plain but adequate, running to potatoes prepared in a variety of exotic forms. Breakfast was invariably bread and butter soaked in bowls of coffee. I was surprised to find that these folks suffered no shortage of good fresh butter, but then supposed René got it from his dairy friends.

Tobacco posed a problem. It was strictly rationed, and since my host didn't seem to have any special contacts in this line, he had to get by on his meager ration of the stuff. The ration was about twenty cigarettes a week, as I recall it, and five little cigars about the size of a king-size cigarette. These he firmly insisted on sharing with me fifty-fifty, even to cutting the fifth cigar in half. In England we had experienced absolutely no shortage of smokes. Name brands in the post exchange sold for about five cents a pack, and there was no serious shortage of English brands on the market.

I'd already learned that things were otherwise on the Continent; it was at the little bistro where I got too swacked to ride the tandem that I had my first lesson. As we were having our first glass of wine that morning, before the crowd collected, someone gave me a cigarette. I smoked it down to about an inch, and being finished with it, threw it down and prepared to grind it out with my foot. All eyes were on me in astonishment as René hastily stopped me, picked up the butt, carefully snubbed it out, and put it with a collection of other butts in a little tin he carried in his pocket. Thus I learned that the smallest remnant of a cigarette was hoarded, the bits to be rolled together to make a whole cigarette—whose butt again would be the start of another collection. My unthinking act of throwing that butt down would have been a dead giveaway had the wrong person seen it.

One morning following a night of rain, Mme Méssager and Robert talked excitedly about something they were going to gather in the woods. I understood that it was something to eat, something they considered to be a rare delicacy, but I couldn't understand what it was they were trying to describe. I finally decided that this thing they called "escargot" was some kind of mushroom, and I looked forward to a good dinner. The two went off gaily with a burlap sack and were gone the better part of the morning. I was in the kitchen when they returned, and my hostess emptied out on the floor two dozen large snails, their shells covered with green moss and slime. This was "escargot." And we were to eat them! I shuddered at the prospect, and if the mere sight of those monsters made me skeptical, the preparation of them for eating nauseated me.

Mme Méssager dumped the whole lot of snails, after rinsing them briefly, into a big pot, threw in a handful of salt, turned on the fire, and then called me to watch the fun. The combination of heat and salt spurred the snails, straining out of their shells, to heroic efforts to escape the pot. The shells ranged in size from walnut to small-tangerine, and the running gear of the snails, stretched out in their desperate escape attempts, ran to nearly four inches. Robert and his mother made great sport of knocking the creatures back into the brine, and slowly the combination of heat and salt subdued them. But the slimy corruption that covered the surface of the water was more than I could bear. If I was to eat the things, as I knew politeness mandated, I didn't want to acquire any more ghastly pictures that would run through my head and raise my gorge at dinner. I retreated to the window to monitor traffic in the street.

All too soon, my hostess drew a large platter from the oven and set it on the table. She proudly lifted the cover, and there on the plate were the snail shells, now all clean and shining, with openings turned up and filled with an appetizing-looking stuffing. The snails had been drawn from their shells, prepared with a garlic-butter sauce seasoned with herbs, then stuffed back into the shells. That dish even smelled delicious, and I am sure if it hadn't been for my recollection of the cooking, plus a natural inclination against eating crawling things, I would have thoroughly enjoyed the two or three "mushrooms" I managed to force down.

13

According to René, there were twenty thousand German troops in and around Verdun! The enemy soldiers were well disciplined, he assured me, but alien control was the plain fact of life in the city; and my own delicate position made me acutely aware of the German presence. Columns of armed soldiers marched past the Méssager home every day on their way to field excercises, and almost the only automobiles to be seen in operation were staff cars carrying German officers. Large numbers of German soldiers idled on the streets downtown, I was told, and all through the night I heard the tramp of booted feet and the lusty singing of the patrols as they covered our section of the town—"Hi-lee, hi-lo." Whoosh!

I lived constantly with a sense of danger. It made me jumpy and played weird tricks on my imagination. Seeing the uniformed persons of the enemy every day made me apprehensive, even though I was sure they couldn't see through my disguise. But the real fear came from my dread certainty that a vast, unseen machinery of detection was slowly but surely tracking me down, that the apparently innocuous civilian who'd just passed by after throwing me a second glance was the man who was finally going to grab me. The terrible Gestapo was never out of my mind.

It was quite an experience to stand by the side of the road and watch columns of the enemy walking past, sometimes so close I could have reached out and touched the men. There was a fascination in catching the eyes of occasional soldiers and wondering if the thought was in their minds that perhaps I was not a Frenchman. I was dressed in old working clothes and had replaced my own shoes with a pair of René's castoffs. But the feeling persisted that my foreignness stuck out all over me and must be obvious to anyone who looked closely enough.

These German soldiers looked damned good, even in their fatigue uniforms. They were strong and tanned, carried themselves well, and handled their well-kept weapons with a deadly assurance. I was most impressed by their stimulating marching songs and was amazed to see troops singing on their way to and from the tedium of field drills. René told me they sang only because they were ordered to, but even that did not dispel my feeling that these soldiers had the highest morale of any I had ever encountered.

One day Robert and I, on our daily trek to their garden, were stopped at a road by a column of troops passing by. It looked to be about a company, with breaks of thirty yards between platoons. I was pushing the wheelbarrow, loaded with seed potatoes, while Robert carried the garden tools. We watched for a bit while the column marched by, and when we spotted a gap coming up that would permit us to cross the road, we started across, Robert ahead of me. I had just got to the middle of the road when I heard a shout followed by a scurrying and a rattling of hardware. My blood froze and the hair went up on my neck, because all this excitement meant only one thing to me: I had been discovered! I stopped dead and glanced to my left, whence the soldiers were coming, but they had all dispersed off the road, no doubt to surround me. I glanced to my right: The unit that had just passed had set up a light machine gun, aimed directly at me and placed not twenty yards away.

I was petrified—too stunned to make a move, able only to wait and wonder dully why they didn't shoot or close in.

Then someone shouted another order, and the column of soldiers re-formed as quickly as it had scattered.

It was probably an air-attack practice dispersal. Before the soldiers resumed marching, I had the wit to move quickly out of the way; I kept moving down the path without looking back. The experience shook me pretty badly, but young Robert thought it was a great joke.

Shortly after my arrival at the Méssagers', René explained to me that I had to have an identity card, as plans were afoot to have me escorted out of the country. This card had to bear the signature of the prefecture of police, and it had to have my picture on it. In view of the remarkable tales I had heard of the French underground, the provision of an identity card didn't seem to me to be an extraordinary undertaking.

When René announced one morning—it was the eleventh of May—that we were going to have my picture taken, I assumed that we would slip in the back door of some clandestine photography studio and that everything would be done in the best melodramatic style. Off we went; but I was completely unprepared when René signaled that we were to stop (the tandem again) in front of a large department store in the main downtown district. He parked the bicycle and led me into the store, close to the entrance of which was a "picture-while-you-wait" apparatus operated by a good-looking young girl. I was appalled! German soldiers stood ahead of me in the line, and very soon they were queued up behind me; and I could see them, in assorted uniforms, walking around the floor of the store.

I was scared and angry—angry at René for exposing me this way, and deathly afraid of having to speak with the operator, or of failing suspiciously in following instructions I might not understand. But I shuffled on toward my turn, and when I arrived at the booth she smiled, sat me down, and urged me to smile. All four exposures, when they were produced, reflected my state of mind. They showed a drawn, tense face and wide, scared eyes. A smile on *that* face would have looked like a death smirk. When we had the pictures, we strolled casually—in René's case—out of the store, got on the bicycle, and pedaled away. And it was from there that my irrepressible host took me on a tour of the city.

René had repeatedly assured me, as the days wore on, that arrangements were being made to turn me over to the underground to be spirited out of the country. We talked of this often, but he would never tell me specifically what he was doing about it and I didn't press him. On the evening of my third day in Verdun, René simply handed me the card. There I was, signed, sealed, and delivered: "Jean Humbert, *méchanicien*"—mechanic. This was the all-important *carte d'identité* that everyone carried and had to show on demand. René also announced that arrangements had been made for me to leave on the fifteenth (three days hence), but he did not know the destination. I was to be interviewed on the next morning by a woman whom he described only as one who could help me.

At the appointed hour the following morning, we cycled up to a small apartment building in the downtown section of Verdun. I was shown up to an apartment on the second floor, and René presented me to the lady who came to the door. Then he left, to return later. The woman was in her early or middle thirties, attractive, and quite pleasant. I recall little of the conversation, but I wondered at the time how this gentle female could be part of the underground. I repeated the general facts bearing upon my situation, showed her the pictures of my family, and tried to do all the things I thought were expected of me to establish my identity. After what seemed an inconclusive hour, René reappeared and we took our leave. I still didn't know where I was to be taken; maybe I wouldn't be taken at all.

The woman had been satisfied about me, however, and René was instructed to have me prepared to leave as planned, on the fifteenth. He had been told in some detail just what was to be done, so in the short time remaining we went about our preparations with considerable relief on both sides. I gave up all remnants of my uniform, including my underwear. In their place René provided an ancient but passable suit, a French-type flannel shirt with tails that reached to my knees, and a beret. At my request Mme Méssager sewed my dog tags to the inner soles of my new socks, because I felt that in the event of recapture I should have at least some evidence of my military identity. I left my pictures with René, since they all had English writing on them. I felt well disguised and ready to go.

However, during the morning of the day before I was to leave, Robert and I stood outside and watched a large formation of American heavy bombers pass high overhead, so high we could see the planes only occasionally, when the sunlight glanced off their silver bodies. That evening René learned that the American heavies we had seen in the morning had smashed the railroad marshaling yards at Epinal, temporarily disrupting all traffic through the town. My route to "destination unknown" was through Epinal, so my departure had to be postponed. This was the first I knew that I would be traveling by train.

The next two days were trying ones for me. The letdown after learning of the postponement, combined with my increasing uneasiness that too many people knew of my presence, put me on edge. To make matters worse, shortly after lunch on the fifteenth, the day I was to have left, René explained that I would have to stay in my room that afternoon, that someone might be coming who must not see me. For the first time during my stay, my host looked worried, so my uneasiness increased.

Someone eventually did come, a man and a woman, and in the course of a long palaver, voices were raised angrily. It was maddening to have to stay quiet in that room, unable to do anything. It seemed that with escape almost within my grasp, I was trapped. But the contentious duo went away finally, and the tension seemed to ease in the evening. René did not explain to me what the talk was about, but my mind delivered up the notion of greedy relatives putting the screws on my host to give me up, get a reward, and ingratiate himself with the German authorities.

The next day René announced that my departure had been fixed for the following afternoon. So that evening, the sixteenth—thirteen days after my bail-out—he briefed me carefully on what I was to do. The pleasant lady who had interviewed me the week before would come in a car and take me to the station, buy me a certain magazine from the news kiosk, and stand me in a certain part of the waiting room. Another woman would come up to me at about four o'clock, greet me as "Jean Humbert," and take me in tow. I was to be a distant relative; please try to act like one, René instructed me. From there on I was to do exactly as told, keep my mouth shut, and hope for the best.

We spent the evening winding up preparations. René rechecked my clothes and few personal belongings to make sure there were no telltale signs; admonished me on a thousand and one things I should or should not do; speculated anew on how the war would go. The next morning we were up early, and after breakfast there was an interminable, unnerving wait. This was a turning point: I was about to leave the hospitality of an ordinary French citizen and enter into the charge of the "organization." I had visions of a terrifyingly spectacular swoop by the Gestapo just as we were to get on the train.

At last René, who was watching at the window, announced that there was a car out front. I gathered my gear, put on my beret, and we all trooped downstairs and out to the car. In the best French tradition, I kissed my host and hostess, shook hands with a solemn Robert, and was hustled into the car. We were driven straight to the station, my contact woman and I, and upon arrival she told the driver to wait while she escorted me inside. She was very nervous and seemed anxious to get rid of me and be on her way. She stood me in the proper place, bought me the proper magazine, and after a hasty *"Bonne chance!"* left me.

Standing there alone I felt as though a great weight had been lifted from me. I had been too long tied in one place, with an ever-greater number of people aware of my presence, many of whom must have suspected something irregular about me. This not only increased my chances of being apprehended, but also, more terrible to think about, meant increasing danger to René, his family, and probably his friends. Now that that responsibility was gone, I felt a measure of peace and calm as I stood by a wall of the station and watched the people hurrying about.

14

I hadn't waited long before I was accosted by an electric wisp of a woman fully six inches shorter than I. She looked to be in her late forties, and she had eyes sunk deep in a face drawn with fatigue. She inquired, "Jean Humbert?" and when I nodded, she kissed me briskly on the cheek, assured herself that I was all assembled and ready to go, then directed me to wait while she went after my ticket.

Once again my hopes of association with a glamorous woman of the French underground were dashed. This woman was old enough to be my mother, and was also one of the curtly decisive sort of women I'd always found annoying. Mme Raymonde—for that was the name I was to know her by—returned, handed me a ticket, and told me to follow her. I imitated her way of displaying the ticket as we went through the inspection gate, and she led me directly to a third-class car on a train standing at the platform. I followed her as she elbowed and pushed her way to seats in a crowded compartment, and sat down with considerable relief. Shortly the train pulled out and we were on our way.

As I studied Mme Raymonde, seated opposite me in the compartment, I wondered how on earth this woman proposed to ease me by all the obstacles this trip would entail, to wherever it was we were going. She hardly appeared physically capable of getting herself downtown and back.

She was small-boned and narrow-shouldered and looked like under ninety pounds of badly worn humanity. And when she sat sleeping with her head thrown back and her mouth open, as she did frequently, she looked witless in the bargain.

This odd little woman wore carelessly assembled clothing of mousey gray and black, and avoided being dowdy only by being so small. Her gray-black hair, most of it, was pulled straight back from her face and fastened up near the crown of her head in a "there-dammit-that'll-hold-you" sort of a bun. She had the thin, delicate hands of a very old woman, hands that were always doing something—writing, gesticulating, or clutching a large, worn handbag while their mistress sat in open-mouthed slumber.

But if Mme Raymonde looked pathetic while she slept, she looked the opposite when awake. When I conjure up her face in my mind, it is an angry face, condemning and protesting passionately. For awake she was either violently and vocally angry or (as her narrowed eyes and pursed lips revealed) silently thinking about being angry. She treated me indifferently, as though I were someone else's small boy she was dutifully looking after for a while on a visit to an uncle in the next town. Only twice that I can recall did she look at me with any sense of recognition during the four days I was in her company. But I noticed that she looked at everyone, even those she was addressing, as though she were seeing just through and beyond them to the object of her anger.

And her anger at the Germans and the German occupation was monumental; I am certain it was the sole source of strength for the moral and physical exertions of which I was the present beneficiary. She was the twentieth-century reincarnation of the Paris women of the barricades, screaming defiance at tyranny. I sat appalled many a time as this stick of congealed anger would come awake and begin haranguing the occupants of our compartment. It was not difficult, even for one as inept at French as I was, to understand who was the object of her invective, and I worried that she would bring the authorities down on us.

But my distrust of this formidable woman disappeared in the course of that first day as it became obvious that she knew precisely what she was doing. Her casual contempt for danger was matched by a capacity for steering clear of it. Nevertheless, it was unnerving to have to sit there clutching my French picture magazine and hear her denouncing the Boche to a compartmentful of sinister strangers.

Even though by evening of that first day Mme Raymonde had won my confidence completely, she shook me rigid by one stunt she pulled. Having been cautioned to the greatest discretion and complete silence lest my accent betray me, I considered everyone around me to be dangerous, and officials of the railroad especially so. At one stop late that first night my guide and I got off the train and walked across a dark and deserted waiting room toward a gate where an official checked tickets. Mme Raymonde, several paces ahead as usual, said something to the official and walked on.

I tried to breeze past with a casual nod and a smile, but he stopped me by taking hold of my arm. He said something I didn't understand, so I shrugged my shoulders, thinking, "This is the way it happens. Some simple thing I don't comprehend, and probably could have avoided, trips me up!" I was already marshaling my resources to make a break for it when Mme Raymonde came back and said merely, *"Américain!"* with a jerk of her head in my direction. I was astounded, both by the fact that she had spoken our terrible secret out loud in so public a place as a railroad station, and by the French official's reaction. He released me immediately with a nod of his head that showed that it was, in that case, all right.

We went to a cafe and ate a plain supper in silence, and while I dawdled over coffee, Mme Raymonde occupied herself writing in a little notebook she had fished out of her grab-bag purse. She was oblivious of me as she wrote, and gave only the most perfunctory attention to a tall, pleasant-looking young man with a shock of brown wavy hair who joined us at our table. The newcomer was evidently expected, because after a time all three of us left the cafe together, returned to the station, and shortly thereafter boarded another train. Sometime after midnight we came to the town of Nancy, and once more we left the train, this time to sit for a while in a waiting room. There Mme Raymonde procured three mugs of ersatz coffee, and in the course of our four-hour wait I became acquainted with the newcomer, whose name was Paul. Mme Raymonde spoke a little English, and Paul, who spoke both French and German well, was willing to slow his French down to where I could manage it.

Paul was an Alsatian who had been drafted two years earlier into the German air force, in whose ranks he served as a radio technician at Schipol, the huge air base near Amsterdam. When he learned that his parents had been "resettled" from their farm in Alsace to an unnamed place in Poland, Paul made plans to desert. He first divorced his wife, who was living in Paris with relatives, so that his actions would not bring reprisals upon her. He then skipped out, and by some means he did not explain to me, arranged to tie up with Mme Raymonde as another passenger on the underground railroad out of France. He was a relaxed, easygoing, pleasant companion, with an air of studied gentleness about him. He was not interested in discussing the war or the Germans, preferring instead to swap jokes with me.

I took the occasion of this relaxed interlude to ask Mme Raymonde how she knew her way around so well, apparently with no fear of being stopped by Vichy French railroad officials or by the police.

"My husband worked on the railroads a long time," she replied, "and I know many railroad people. I have made this trip ten times already this year. One knows what to do, and one is warned by friends who is to be trusted and when the Gestapo is near."

For a change, I noticed, she was looking at me instead of through me as she talked. And although the light from the single naked bulb hanging from the ceiling gave her drawn face a deathly cast, there seemed to be an expression of gentleness there I had not seen before. Or perhaps it was her voice, or what she said, that gave me that impression.

"I have a son the same age as you. You are about twenty-six, no?" she went on. "My only son. He went to Africa when the Boche came, and now he fights with the Americans in Italy. I have had no word from him for two months."

I took this occasion to express my hope of getting to Spain so that I could very quickly rejoin my squadron in England and get back into the shooting.

"But it is much safer in Switzerland, and much closer," she replied.

"One is not safe until one is dead," I answered. "While there is a war, I must do what I can to help the fighting. Paul says the Americans fly their soldiers out of Switzerland, those who escape there. Is this true?"

"I have heard the same thing," she answered, but without conviction. "Anyway, one can get into Switzerland, but the Boche guard the Spanish border very carefully. We shall see."

I disliked leaving the question up in the air this way, but decided not to press my guide further just then. She seemed to have enough burdens on her thin shoulders without added worry. We talked until Mme Raymonde stated she wished to sleep for a while. Paul took the cue and stretched himself out on one of the benches that served in lieu of chairs at our table. He suggested that I do likewise, since we would be another two or three hours in the place.

I was still curious about this thin, intense female and was reluctant to pass up a chance to learn more about her. I had no real understanding of her purpose in making these trips, but I was certain that guiding strays like Paul and me was incidental to some other business. It occurred to me that perhaps she simply followed her husband about on his runs as a railroad man; she had said he was an engineer. With no family to look after, this seemed to me to be a plausible explanation for her traveling.

So just as she was about to settle down to sleep, her head cradled in her arms on the table, I asked her if her husband was an engineer on the line we were riding. She raised her head to look at me out of weary eyes.

"My husband died three months ago," she said. "American planes strafed the locomotive he was driving, and he was killed when it exploded." With that she put her head down and went to sleep.

15

Mme Raymonde roused Paul and me in the gray chill of early morning. After hot coffee, we returned to the platform and boarded another train. Like the others we had been riding, this was a third-class local. At each stop the train became more and more crowded; by eight o'clock the compartments were full and people stood in the aisles.

In the course of the morning I was forced to heed an increasingly urgent call of nature. I disliked the risk of moving about in the train, but there was no choice. I leaned over to my guide, who sat opposite me, and whispered, "Latrine?" She asked, "*C'est nécessaire?*" and the fervor of my "*Absolument!*" convinced her that it probably was. She went out and scouted the car for me, then reported the location of the restroom. She told me to take my magazine along. When I had finally battled my way through the crowded aisle to the door between the cars—feeling "At last!"—I was nearly frantic on finding a line of eight or ten people waiting a turn at the toilet.

I am not a line bucker, but on this occasion I racked my brain for some way of beating what looked like a long wait for something that must happen considerably sooner. But I had not reckoned on the wretchedness of third-class accommodations. As I was soon to discover, the little cabinet was highly aromatic and unhygienic, and it would be hard to imagine anyone's wanting to tarry there. The line moved rather briskly.

Before long I was next at the door, thinking that in a few minutes things would again be right with the world, when a bumptious, professorial-looking little fellow wearing a homburg and a goatee tried to muscle in ahead of me, making what were probably plausible explanations in French, which I could not understand. A reasonable discretion would have cautioned me to let the little guy go ahead, but circumstances almost out of control forced discretion aside. As the professor was making his explanation, the door to the toilet opened, and as the occupant stepped out, I pushed the interloper aside, stepped through the door, and locked it. Never before or since has simple privacy been so welcome to me. The little man was not in sight when I emerged, and I got back to my seat without further incident.

The second day's travel was much like the first, with our train spending much of the time on sidings as both freight and through passenger trains passed us by, and with the population of our compartment changing with each of the many stops. These were the ordinary people of France who shared our compartment, identifiable by their drab, worn clothing; by their uniform look of weariness; and by their smell. With some relief, I noted two other things about those French people: They all liked to talk, but none cared particularly about listening. This was fortunate, because I found that complete strangers who addressed me didn't seem to give a damn that I never replied. For them talking seemed to be in a class with gum chewing—a purely subjective process requiring no outside help for its enjoyment.

My seat by the compartment window gave me a good vantage point from which to view the narrow strip of France we passed through. I saw what had been done to the marshaling yards at Epinal by those American bombers Robert Méssager and I had watched passing over Verdun four days earlier. Two locomotives still lay on their sides across the way, one resting across the other. Steel rails were tortuously twisted, one of them pointing crookedly at the sky. The whole area was a cluttered, plowed-up shambles. Knifing cleanly through the whole mess, however, were two spanking new sets of tracks that had been laid and were carrying traffic eight hours after the raid.

I noticed with some uneasiness that in spite of concerted Allied efforts to disrupt rail traffic, things seemed to be moving along pretty well. Even then, only a scant few weeks before the invasion, when interdiction had been stepped up, there appeared to be no restrictions on train travel. And by and large the trains were in pretty good shape. The lowly local we were traveling in was reasonably comfortable, and a sight cleaner than some first-class trains I had ridden in the States before the war. And the first-class trains I saw from our sidings were marvels to behold. They showed a sheen and a luxury I hadn't seen anywhere else, and my glimpses of the sleek, beautiful women and carefully groomed German officers who populated these luxury coaches again made me question my ability to tell the real from the unreal.

As we stopped at one station along the way, I sat next to the window away from the platform. My gaze wandered across the empty space to the people on the opposite platform, only a few yards away, and stopped idly on one group. A woman was crying into a handkerchief, and a man at her side was comforting her. On either side of the pair was a blank-faced German soldier. It was the fifth person, taller and standing behind the couple, who finally satisfied my curiosity and focused my casual glance until comprehension froze me with the terrible meaning of what I saw. For this fifth person was an American airman.

I had missed the details of his clothing at first, but there was no mistaking the olive drab trousers, the cut of the leather jacket, even the GI shoes. He was hatless, but had a soiled, bloody bandage around his head.

I stared across the short space that separated us and felt this American's thoughts crawl up my back and burn my neck. There before me, manifest in three tragic figures and their captors, was the reward for patriotism, for ordinary human compassion for a fellow man in distress. It was an eloquent tableau, and I knew that there, but for the grace of God, stood the Méssagers and I.

About the middle of the afternoon of the second day out of Verdun, we got off the train at a town called Lure, just thirty miles from the Swiss border. We walked through quaint, quiet streets to a modest residential section right on the edge of town. At one of the houses, Mme Raymonde motioned us to stop, went on through the gate, and knocked. The knock was answered by an elderly lady who welcomed Mme Raymonde warmly. She was not at all surprised to learn of Paul's identity or mine, so I presumed that she was part of the underground. She immediately set out coffee, bread, and some cold cuts.

When we had finished eating, Paul, after a brief discussion with our hostess, asked me if I would care to take a little walk. We were right on the edge of town, so we would stroll up the hill that rose a little way behind this house and cut some grass for the woman's rabbits. I welcomed Paul's suggestion, since we hadn't had much chance to move about for the past twenty-four hours.

It was a beautiful evening, the sun just setting and the sky flecked with rose-bottomed clouds. Paul and I walked up a little path to the crown of the hill and looked out over the town. I would have thoroughly enjoyed the peaceful vista had we not noticed two German soldiers walking up the path toward us. We went to work cutting grass and stuffing it into the bag we had brought along, and as the soldiers came closer, I was relieved to notice that they were unarmed. As they walked by I didn't dare look up, but Paul returned their greeting. His manner and tone did not invite conversation, and after a brief pause the pair continued on their way. Paul looked over at me and chuckled to see sweat on my forehead.

We three travelers shared a sitting room that night, Mme Raymonde sleeping on the couch and Paul and I rolled up in blankets on the floor. Our guide called us awake the next morning at about sunup, and in the dim, early-morning light it pleased me to see that Mme Raymonde looked rested and refreshed for the first time in our short association. She sat up, and when her feet found the small felt slippers, she stood up and moved to the window and jerked the blackout drapes aside. Her face gladdened perceptibly at the sight of the faultless May morning, and she opened the windows to breathe deeply of the washed, early-morning air. She closed her eyes, as though she couldn't stand to both see and smell so much beauty at one and the same time.

After a few moments of deep breathing, she opened her eyes, allowed herself a soupçon more of looking at rosy puffs of cloud, then replaced her mask as she closed the windows and walked to a round table, where her purse rested. She sat down, reached a small mirror from its place in the purse, and propped it up against the lamp base. In the same sure manner she retrieved a large comb from the purse and set it on the table.

Sitting straight in her chair, Mme Raymond removed the six hairpins that secured the bun at the crown of her head and allowed a cascade of gray-black hair to fall to just below her shoulders. Thus framed, her face, with no change in her mask, became feminine and vulnerable, but her eyes gave the fact no recognition. She picked up her comb and began pulling it through her hair, carefully, methodically, smoothing the path of each stroke with her left hand.

Her expression never changed, but in her motions of combing and smoothing there was a luxuriating, an enjoyment of caring for herself. Unhurried and careful though it was, the combing was done in just a few minutes. Then the hands, operating as automatically as though they had no directing from their mistress, sorted out tresses and twisted them, pulling them gently taut, inserting hairpins as required, until abruptly the cascade was recaptured in a now neat bun at the crown of her head. Very close inspection might have revealed that some strands and locks of hair were not as securely fastened as others and would, within the hour, get free to give Mme Raymonde's coiffure its characteristic go-to-hell look.

After the usual bread-and-coffee breakfast, we gave thanks to our hostess and were on our way, Mme Raymonde in

the lead as usual, with Paul and me bumbling along in her
wake. I was so accustomed by now to complete ignorance
about what we were up to that it no longer worried me. If
our guide had suddenly handed me a pogo stick and announced that we were to hop the next leg to Sardinia, I
would have gone bouncing off without a question. The
night's sleep had restored me and my usual faith in the
rightness of things, whatever might develop.

Straight to the station we steamed, but just short of the
arched entryway Mme Raymonde seemed to change her
mind and we went on up the street without a change of
pace. When we were about a block past the station, she
stopped, spoke briefly to Paul, and pointed to a cafe across
the street. I was puzzled by the proceedings, especially
when I saw Paul's eyebrows go up at what Mme Raymonde
said.

She left us then to go back to the station, and Paul and I
slanted across to the cafe. I asked him, "What's up?" but
he signaled me to be quiet. We took a table at the rear of
the nearly deserted cafe, and after Paul had ordered coffee
for the two of us, I put my question again. He answered
with one barely whispered word: "Gestapo." We had nearly
walked into one of the secret-police dragnets set up to trap
just such people as Paul and me—and Mme Raymonde.

16

Gestapo! How, I asked Paul, had Mme Raymonde known
they were in the station? He shrugged. "They have means
of warning each other, *la Resistance*." We sat, mostly
silent, for the better part of an hour, our coffee grown cold
before us in the cups, each engrossed in his own speculations.
When Mme Raymonde appeared, she was her usual matter-
of-fact self. She had a small glass of wine, then marched us
off to the station and onto our train. She did not even
mention the interruption, as though even this close call
with the Boche was unworthy of her protracted attention.

We arrived at Belfort, the end of our train travels, about
noon, having covered about 150 miles in two days. Not too
bad, considering that our trains had stopped at every station along the way, and had negotiated one badly bombed
marshaling yard in the bargain. Once out of the station at
Belfort, Paul and Mme Raymonde went into a huddle,
following which Paul waved casually to me and sauntered
off down the street. I thought from his manner that he had
gone off on some errand, but as my diminutive guide and I
went on about our mysterious affairs, I came to the conclu-
sion that we had seen the last of the Alsatian. I was sorry,
because I had developed a real liking for this friendly
fellow who bore his troubles so lightly.

Mme Raymonde and I rode in a hired car from Belfort to

the little town of Delle, close to the Swiss border, and after some unexplained hithering and thithering there, we took another car out into the country. We went several miles out, turned onto a little country road, and pulled up before a farm establishment set somewhat back from the road. My guide paid the driver, and then led me up to the house, her manner revealing that she was no stranger here. She rapped on the shabby door, and it was opened by a large young man with untidy blonde hair who greeted Mme Raymonde and motioned us both into the house.

We were led to a cellar room of the house by this coarse-looking young fellow, and there we found a group of about seven people of assorted ages. The place buzzed with flies and smelled of unwashed people, untrained dogs, and stale cabbage. Besides the fellow who answered our knock, there was a roly-poly *maman* who continually occupied herself with handing out plates of unappetizing-looking food covered with flies; two other brutish young men; a chubby young girl about fifteen years old with black-edged teeth who took an immediate shine to me; a young boy of eight; and two little children with runny noses and no clear indication as to their sex.

Throughout the afternoon there was continuous coming and going. With a whole house apparently available, I could not understand why everyone chose to congregate in this one small room where the flies lived; but they did, and it became unbearably stuffy. My guide seemed to know these people pretty well, and so it was my good fortune for the first half-hour to be ignored by all except the flies and the leering little female. As the conversation eddied around me, I watched two of the young men as they postured before Mme Raymonde, who listened to their braggadocio with amused interest. They both had large pistols stuck in their waistbands, and one of them flashed an enormous wad of bills. They also displayed a number of watches. Through what I could understand of the conversation and from what I could see, I supposed that these fellows were smugglers operating across the Swiss border.

I knew that eventually the fat *maman* would get around

to offering me some of the slop that the others were sharing with the flies, and I tried to steel myself, knowing I should eat whenever I had the chance. I think I was mentally prepared to have a try at it, but during a lull in the conversation, and while *Maman* was out at the garbage pail fixing me a plate, the blond lout, standing in the middle of the room, lifted a leg and broke wind noisily. Black-tooth laughed delightedly, and the little boy made some remark that brought on more laughter.

Taking advantage of this bucolic diversion, I slipped out the door and sat on the ground outside in the shade, my back against the wall of the house. No one seemed to notice my exit except my unattractive admirer, who emerged shortly with her buzzing satellites and, settling herself a short distance from me, began to repair a bicycle tire. For once I was thankful for her presence; she attracted the flies from me. It was no trouble at all resisting the display of thigh and breast aimed at me, especially since the more she displayed, the greater the attraction for the flies.

Around the middle of the afternoon Paul put in an appearance. I shook hands with him and showed him down into the stinking rendezvous. He exchanged a few words with Mme Raymonde, politely refused a plateful of trash from *Maman,* and sat down; he was ignored by the young men just as I had been. He was able to tell me that after dark we would go off with part of this riffraff and walk across the border into Switzerland. From what I had seen of this crew, I didn't have much faith in their company, so I suggested to Paul that we might do better by ourselves. He told me then that the border was closely guarded by the Germans, that there was some special alert on, and that these contraband runners knew the safest routes to guide us past the border patrols.

As the afternoon crept on, I more and more urgently had to go to the john. I asked Paul if he knew where the latrine was, but he shrugged and asked *Maman.* She gave me a snaggle-toothed grin and bawled for someone. When the young girl put her head in the door, *Maman* instructed her to show me the way, and I made my exit, red-faced, to the accompaniment of much snickering.

The wench led me to the barn and showed me a privy arrangement tacked to the side of the building as a sort of lean-to. The only privacy was provided by a half-length burlap cloth that hung in the doorway, but it concealed little as it waved freely outward in the afternoon breeze, just out of reach of the person ensconced on the crude two-holer. And that miserable female took up her tire repairing on the barn floor in front of the burlap, so what with the rough edges of the seat and the solicitous watchfulness of that girl, my stay there was a brief one.

Along in the late afternoon, the activity in the cellar began to take some direction as with considerable to-do packs were made up, some assorted equipment assembled, and the prospective travelers became distinct from the nontravelers. Among the former were two late arrivals I noticed particularly. One was a really lovely, trim little brunette in her early or middle twenties, who, I learned later, was a schoolteacher by profession. The other was a tall young chap who stood out from the other fellows because he was clean and reserved and had a look of intelligence about him. This lad arrived fitted out with a large, cloth-covered wooden case. Strapped so it could be carried like a knapsack, it contained tins that rattled every time the case was jarred.

It was still two hours before dark on this clear, balmy evening when, amid a great deal of clatter and chatter, the crowd formed up to begin its trek. I was aghast to see our leader, one of the armed bumpkins, lead out straight across an open meadow toward a wood about half a mile away. This put us in full view of the road running past the farmhouse and another running parallel to our course. Paul spoke to the lead man and urged either that we move a little less openly or that we wait until after dark. Nothing came of the suggestion as on we went, a dozen people strung out over fifty yards, loaded with packs and led by two armed thugs. I doubted that we would get through the first hour unchallenged.

When we came to the copse at the far side of the meadow, we made our way to a small clearing well into the trees and there assembled. The two ruffians then ordered us to wait while they went on, evidently to reconnoiter. We ranged ourselves in a rough circle on the grass, lounged on our packs, and prepared to wait. I took the opportunity to strike up a conversation with the young French girl, who seemed so out of place in this mongrel company. It had occurred to me that if she was going to spend any time in Switzerland, she would make mighty good company, and I figured to get a running start.

But her reaction to my approach was unexpected, to say the least. "You are an American pilot, no?" she asked right off, and when I modestly allowed that I was, thinking this was a good beginning, she went on, "But why do you drop your bombs on French people, eh? This is cruel, the killing of old people and children who have no wish for the war! Why do you bomb the cities where there are no German soldiers?" Her dark eyes flashed and she gestured violently as she talked.

She went on and on, telling about the bombing of her town only a week before, of the terror, the pain, and suffering. At first I was angry at this unreasonable girl, but as she talked on I began to see things in quite a different light.

I guess that up until then I had blandly assumed that our bombs, being Allied bombs, had a magic property that somehow made them acceptable to the French civilians who were inadvertently blasted. But now I pictured myself standing in Epinal with this girl, with Mme Raymonde, with the numberless worn French people I had seen on the train, watching the Flying Fortresses, high up, dropping their lethal specks, hearing the sirens, scurrying frantically for cover. And then hearing and feeling the shouting thunder, the racking blast upon blast that tore the day apart. And finally the screams and sobs giving tongue to the wreckage. It is an unsettling experience to realize suddenly that you, even you, could come to hate your own people for what

hey do, however good their intentions. I had no reply for
he girl, only listened quietly until she was spent.

Once she'd relented and the evening wore on, we became quite friendly. However, our stops after this first one
were brief and infrequent, so I was not able to learn much
about this lovely girl.

We waited in the circle for about an hour, and although I
was impatient to get under way, it was not unpleasant in
he woods that warm, clear afternoon, especially following
he farmhouse stay. When our leaders returned, there was
some palaver and thrashing of arms, after which we shoul-
dered our packs and went off in trail. I lost all sense of
direction very shortly, since we were in deep woods, so
had I been left to my own devices, I would have had no
idea which way to go. But during the first part of that trek I
didn't much care where we were going, because we were in
he most beautiful forest I have ever seen.

It was a forest of large trees completely clear of underbrush, a spacious woodland of serene majesty. The late sun
sent occasional shafts of light through an almost solid cover
of leaves, and the effect was an amber-green glow that gave
a soft, lovely substance to the air, a glow that seemed to be
generated by the trees, or by the air itself. The rare splashes
of direct sunlight, garish by contrast, emphasized the ethe-
real beauty of the forest.

Thus the first hour or so of our fugitive journey was for
me one of those precious interludes when nature conspires
to present the senses with a mood of exquisite tranquility.
Every sight, every bird call, the woodland scent, seemed
artlessly contrived to transport the beholder. Even time, as
if entranced by the hushed beauty of the place, seemed for
a space reluctant to move on. But the mood, like the sound
of a chorale diminishing to silence, subtly transformed itself until, with the last remnants of evening light about us,
we halted for rest and refreshment in a graying, musty
glade.

17

We stopped only long enough to eat some cold meat, cheese and bread washed down with a few swallows of sour red wine from a communal bottle. As we were about to resume our journey, we learned that the quiet lad with the pack of canned goods was quite sick. He didn't complain to anyone, but Mme Raymonde found him over by a tree retching his insides out, scarcely able to stand. Since there was evidently no choice for him but to move on, I volunteered to carry his pack. My own miserable bundle was no impediment, so I took on his pack, as much to pay my way on the expedition as out of sympathy for this stranger. And that's how I came by the ungainly load on my back, whose clattering at my every blunder and fall through the following four sightless hours made it seem like an obscene monkey from hell, sent up to ride me as a punishment for my sins.

It became dark quickly after we got under way again, and I was soon reminded that I had absolutely no night vision. At first the going was not too bad, because the undergrowth was still light, and by holding lightly to Paul's pack as he walked before me, I could avoid most of the hazards. But the darker it got, the thicker the brush became and the rougher the ground underfoot. I became entangled in briars I couldn't see; saplings would slip between my groping, outstretched hands and knock me back ward onto my clattering cans; holes would open up beneath my feet and hurl me flat on my face, the cans now crashing madly on my back.

With full darkness upon us there began a night of pitch-black blundering, of clanking and thrashing through endless underbrush, of deadly everlasting spells of silence whose only sounds were the drum-thumping of my heart and the chilling, fearsome voices of the dogs used by the German border guards. The contrast between the peacefulness of the early evening walk and the pandemonium of those next four hours was complete.

Once, after I had gone for perhaps twenty paces without a mishap and was allowing myself to hope we would soon be out of this nightmarish forest, I found no ground under my stepping foot and pitched headlong down a fifteen-foot bank. The dirt was soft, so I was not hurt, but I was certain that everyone within a half-mile radius must have paused to look up and wonder at the cause of such a racket. I rolled to a stop amid a paralyzed silence.

For minutes that seemed to stretch into hours, this desert silence enveloped the world, and I found myself holding my breath lest I violate it. We had come to one of the patrol paths, running along close to the foot of the embankment, that laced this border forest; and although the others had been cautioned by a whispered word about the bank and the need for quiet, I had not understood the cue. Beyond that dead silence about us was the distant belling of the dogs. Paul had told me during the afternoon that the German border guards used fierce dogs specially trained to assist their patrols. It is one thing to know such a fact, however, and quite another to lie blind at midnight at the side of a patrol path and hear their blood-chilling baying.

But nothing happened, and after a bit I heard the others walking across the open trail, so I got up and staggered after them. The rest of our trek was more of the same. Each step became a conscious experience, a total preoccupation, its consummation being its only reward. Time was an endless quagmire that, for some reason now obscured, had to be battled. The crashing, clattering, blundering stretches were punctuated by those occasional silences whose form was the distant, deadly dog voices, and whose content was fear.

Somehow we were suddenly bunched at the edge of a wide field. The everlasting woodland, dense to its very edge, gave way to a cultivated field, and looking out through the parted bushes, I found, there in the starlight, that I could actually see. There was an animated debate, with everyone but me talking, as we paused timidly at the edge of darkness: Were we, or were we not, now in Switzerland? I was certain that we were by now in Czechoslovakia.

In the course of this discussion we filtered willy-nilly out of the woods onto the plowed field, I to get away from that accursed forest and the others to give themselves more room to semaphore while with increasing frenzy they talked themselves into believing that we were indeed in Switzerland. I surrendered the backpack to the young man, who had somehow gotten through the trek OK. I should have been dog-tired by that time, but my relief at being out of that brambled hell was so great that I felt downright gay. I grabbed the French girl, who had come over to me to see how I'd fared, and waltzed her around in a circle. Even Mme Raymonde, who had literally led me by the hand through the last hour, caught the spirit and did a little jig.

Switzerland, Austria, or even Germany—I couldn't care less. We were in open country where I could see my way along, where an unobstructed breeze could play through my tattered trousers and soothe my scratched and bruised legs. That, at the moment, was enough for me, and I was not moved to question the consensus of this jibbering congress as to our precise whereabouts.

We eventually proceeded across that open field, which sloped gently upward to a rounded crest a quarter of a mile ahead of us. Once on top of the hill, we could see a wide, easy valley dropping away, and there in the middle distance was a village. On our hilltop another conference was convened, and a parting of the ways decided upon. Mme Raymonde, Paul, and I were to go in one direction, the rest in another. I asked the French girl if I would see her again now that we were in Switzerland, and she said yes, but that I should get in touch with her through Mme Raymonde.

So we separated, and we three, Mme Raymonde in the lead, found a dirt road and walked on in sweet silence. Soon we came to a small group of plain stone buildings, and our guide ordered us to enter the large one. Now exhausted, she spoke her instructions in monosyllables. She entered the door first and turned left into a lighted room. I followed. When my eyes took in the room I froze, shocked by the realization that I had been betrayed. For in the room were half a dozen soldiers in the familiar German Wehrmacht uniforms, some of the men even wearing the unmistakable pot helmets.

✦ PART TWO ✦

Switzerland

18

They looked like Germans, but as I stood in shocked immobility at the door, Mme Raymonde walked to a chair near the wall, sat down, leaned her head back, and went to sleep in one continuous motion. And the soldiers paid no attention to me at all.

So, with Paul up against me wondering at the delay, I looked more closely and saw that they were not Germans after all. Their uniforms, although of German field gray, had neither the fit nor the insignia of Adolf Schicklgruber's troops, and their pot-shaped helmets had a more pronounced flare to the sides and rear than the ones I was familiar with.

Then I saw the sign I would have seen right away except for the shock and my fatigue: the white cross that is the Swiss national emblem. A flag on the wall emblazoned it, and it prominently adorned the uniforms and equipment of the soldiers. I was indeed in Switzerland.

Reassured, I went on into the room, and Paul and I took seats on a bench along the wall. At first I felt pure relief; my world hadn't gone to pieces after all. Then I was annoyed that our guide had brought us directly to the Swiss military, because I had intended making my way to Bern and contacting the Americans there. However, I learned soon enough that as little interest as the American authorities in Switzerland seemed to show in escapees, it made no difference one way or another whether I contacted them directly or never.

After Paul and I had sat there awhile, and my request to be allowed to telephone my people in Bern had been twice refused, one of the soldiers, a little man carrying a long gun and canopied under the flare of his tin hat beckoned us to follow him out of the room. Mme Raymonde, awakened to confer with one of the soldiers, wrote for me on a piece of paper the address in Switzerland at which she could be reached and told me also the alias—Mme Reginald—she used while on the Swiss side.

I had made her promise that at the earliest opportunity after I was established in Switzerland, she would come where I was and be my guest for a real vacation. She would also undertake to relay any messages from me to the young French woman who had accompanied us.

As Paul and I were fussing our gear together preparatory to leaving with the musketeer, Mme Raymonde came over to me, took my hand in hers, and began talking. She knew that I would have preferred a try at the Spanish border, and that I was displeased at being turned in directly to the Swiss. So she undertook to make me see the wisdom of her course.

"You must remember," she was saying, "that your parents and your wife will worry about you. It will be a great comfort to them to know you are safe and well." She paused, looking into my eyes to see if her words had been accepted. She must have seen stubborn remnants of resentment in my face, for she concluded with, "You are brave, *mon cher*, but you are very young!" I kissed her cheek and managed a smile as I bade her au revoir. I knew I was being unreasonable, but despite the gratitude I felt toward this remarkable woman, I remained unhappy at this turn of events.

A month later, when I wrote to Mme Raymonde reminding her of her promise to visit me, my letter was returned with a note from her contact in Switzerland.

"I regret to inform you," the note said, "that Mme Reginald was killed by German soldiers exactly three weeks ago." The letter was dated June 24. Mme Raymonde had died on June 3, just three days before the invasion, as she was going back into France. I made no effort to locate the young woman.

The Swiss soldier led Paul and me out of the building, and directed that we walk to Porrentruy. Although I'd had enough walking for one day, it was pleasant enough to shamble along through the balmy early hours, talking and joking with Paul. We had some fun at the expense of our guard, who plodded ahead of us, his rifle slung and its muzzle covered with a protective rubber cap to keep moisture out. Paul and I talked mainly about our prospects in Switzerland.

I understood that when the Swiss authorities were through with me I would have considerable freedom of movement and plenty of money. In accordance with the Geneva Convention, a soldier who has been captured and subsequently escapes to a neutral country has complete freedom in that country, and is responsible only to the resident representative of his own government. The Geneva Convention notwithstanding, the Swiss had, as a practical matter, to keep Allied escapees confined to a particular area; some ugly incidents between some of our men and German and Japanese diplomatic people in 1942 and 1943 dictated that precaution. So we Allies were restricted to the environs of Montreux, except with express permission from the Swiss police.

I was pleased to reflect that I would receive full pay, including flight pay, for the duration of my internment. Paul was less certain about his status, except that as a ward of the Swiss government he expected to have to work for his keep. He expressed the hope that at the opportune time he could manage to get back to France and join the American or Free French forces.

We walked the full five miles into Porrentruy, and through the sleeping streets of that town to a squat, comic parody of a grim fortress. After some palaver between our Swiss escort and a young corporal, one soldier took me on into the building while another led Paul back out to the street.

This was another farewell, spoken casually on the assumption that Paul and I would see each other again soon. But except for one brief encounter, I saw no more of my gentle Alsatian friend. Much later, when I tried to locate him through the Red Cross, I learned that he had slipped back into France to join the Resistance.

My man led me to a high-ceilinged stone chamber off one of the main passageways. In the dim light I saw a thick layer of straw around the walls of the empty room, and when the guard handed me a coarse wool blanket, I didn't need to be told that the straw was bedding. I was tired and this was Switzerland, so I lay down gladly enough. My sleep was troubled only by some vague dreams of voices, movement, people.

19

woke early the next morning to find my blanket being
shared by two warm bodies pressed on either side of me. I
sat up prepared to be indignant, and found the straw covered with as motley an assortment of characters as any
benign nightmare might provide, some sitting and talking
softly, some still sleeping. The majority of my bedfellows,
including those sharing my blanket, were dark-skinned and
wore a colorful assortment of clothing, including parts of
German military garb. Since about half of the company
wore the characteristic beards and turbans of Sikhs, I assumed that these were British Indian soldiers. Scattered
about in this exotic company were half a dozen Europeans
looking as bewildered as I.

I got up and made my way to the washroom, thinking
that somehow I had been assigned to the wrong place and
should get away. But in the corridor and in the washroom it
was more of the same. Talking in small groups, sitting
silently, cross-legged on cloths performing devotions, washing themselves at the wash trough, placidly combing out
their beards, Indians were all over the place. I was con-
sumed with curiosity, but I couldn't come right out and ask
these people who the hell they were and what the hell they
were doing here. So I approached an Italian officer and
struck up a conversation in French. I told him who I was

and how I came to be there, and asked if he knew who ou
brown companions were. He didn't know, but shortly we
got our answer.

One of the dark-skinned fellows, who had been eaves
dropping on us, came forward and addressed us in very
good English, and as he answered my questions, he un
folded a remarkable tale of misadventure and human courage
These men had, until a few days before, been in a German
POW camp near Epinal in northeast France, sixty miles
from the Swiss border. There had been about six hundred
of them in the Epinal camp, all British colonial troops
captured in various phases of the seesaw battles across
North Africa in 1941 and 1942. All of them had been prison
ers for at least one year, and many had endured some
pretty rough handling.

My narrator, for example, was captured by the Germans
and held under guard in Africa several months. He and the
other prisoners were then committed to Italian care and
transported to a series of camps in Italy, where they were
treated very badly. My friend told me that when the German
officer in Africa announced to his assembled prisoners that
they were being turned over to the Italians, he apologized
to them for this thing he was required to do, and wished
them well. The Italians gained the undying hatred of the
Indians under their charge, because in the Italian camps
these fellows were poorly fed, abused by arrogant guards,
and punished capriciously.

After a year in Italy my friend's group was transported
to a series of camps in France, once again under German
jurisdiction, and they wound up at Epinal late in 1943
There they were used as labor battalions.

On May 14, 1944, the blow fell. A formation of American
heavy bombers, part of the force that destroyed the mar
shaling yards at Epinal and so delayed my departure from
Verdun, bombed the prison camp. More than half the pris
oners were fortunately out on work details that day, but of
those remaining in the camp, my friend estimated that two
hundred were either killed or wounded by the bombardment

For those who were unhurt, the doorway to freedom wa

opened, because the German guard detachment decamped, and for a full day and a half the prisoners were on their own. Some four hundred of them—alone, in pairs, some in groups of up to a dozen—set out for Switzerland, sixty miles away. It must have been a very difficult undertaking for them, since few spoke any French, they were distinctly alien-looking, and they had only the crudest maps if they had any at all. They had only scanty provisions of food to see them through.

I was told later that over 250 of these fellows made it into Switzerland. They hid in the daytime and traveled at night, living off whatever they could find or going hungry. And when this shadow migration reached the Swiss border, it had the alerted German border guard to contend with, reinforced and ready. But these dauntless men pushed through, leaving their own and German dead behind to mark contacts with border patrols.

The story of my Punjabi friend was probably typical. He and four companions were together on a work gang less than a mile from camp when the bombs fell. When their guard left them, they went back into the camp to see what had happened. Having seen, they scrounged what food and belongings could be salvaged and walked out into the hills nearby to plan.

Among their company was a giant Sikh at least six feet four, his powerful body topped by a bearded face and a turban that further exaggerated his size; he was pointed out to me across the room in our Swiss dungeon. Once the five men were back in the hills, the giant recalled that a comrade was locked in the camp jail, condemned to death by a German court martial on a charge of encouraging his fellow prisoners to mutiny. They returned to camp and found the guardhouse still intact, so the giant had to smash the door to release their friend. Back to the hills they went, and straightway the six started their two-day journey for Switzerland.

They had no trouble until they reached the border, but it was their bad luck, while crossing the restricted zone late at night, to run afoul of a patrol of three German soldiers and a dog. As the fugitives crouched in the brush at the side of the patrol path, the Germans came along with their dog on a leash. The Germans were almost abreast of the Indians, some ten yards away, when the dog caught their scent and snarled. The Indians decided to rush the Germans, and the big man made for the dog, which the Germans had released immediately. The soldiers were unslinging their rifles as the six forms broke out of the black shadows into the day-bright moonlight of the trail. The giant caught up the dog as it leaped at him and hurled it yelping at one of the Germans. One of the patrol got his rifle into play and fired once, killing one of the fugitives, but then the giant was upon him, tore the rifle from his hands and, using it as a club, smashed the German's skull with one blow. A second blow killed the dog. The other two soldiers had been overpowered and killed almost before they knew what their danger was.

The Indians took the two good rifles and other useful equipment from the dead soldiers, confirmed that their shot compatriot was indeed dead, and continued their flight. Left behind as they had fallen, still warm and bleeding in the moonlight, were four dead men and the mutilated dog. The giant Sikh still wore dirty, blood-stained bandages on his left arm, a remembrance of his encounter with the animal.

In the middle of the afternoon, upon my return from another round with our Swiss guards (I was still demanding to be allowed to telephone the American officials in Bern), my Punjabi friend, accompanied by the scowling giant, approached me, looking worried, and begged to ask me a question. The big fellow, who spoke no English, had learned I was an American pilot, and he was prepared to wreak vengeance upon me for all his countrymen who had been killed and injured in the bombing of the prison camp.

I made it clear to begin with that I was a *fighter* pilot, not a bomber pilot, hoping that the distinction might help to eliminate me as a subject ripe for vengeance. I then tried to make a case for bombing error, and a bit of lucky guessing straightened that one out too. I explained that there were several German army camps in the vicinity of Epinal, one of which the formation was supposed to bomb. But because of misinformation the Americans had bombed the wrong target, and being so very high up, they could not realize that it was a prison camp they were bombing, since all camps look alike from far above.

This, when fed back in his own language to the big man, satisfied him. I was told that in fact there were several German camps in the vicinity, one of which they knew for certain had not been hit. I expressed sincere regrets on behalf of the U.S. government for the injury done to our fellow soldiers, and added that I was happy that so many of the men had made it safely to Switzerland.

I developed the greatest admiration for these men as soldiers. From what I saw of their behavior, as well as from what they told me of their experiences, I was continually amazed at their thorough military bearing. The presence of so many of them in Switzerland was evidence of their courage, resourcefulness, and determination. In addition, I saw that as soon as they were collected that first day, they identified among their number the man with the highest rank, and although he was only a sergeant, and not very well liked, he nevertheless became the "sergeant major," acting commander of the detachment. He prepared lists of the men, gathered reports on those missing, saw as best he could to those who were injured, and in general ran the outfit. The men obeyed him without question.

Several days later we were all moved by foot to a compound a half-mile away. The Indian sergeant major detailed men of his group to assist, in one case to carry, the injured, and he then formed up the remaining forty or fifty into a column of twos. At the proper time he called the formation to attention and moved them out in an orderly military manner.

Here were men who two or three days previously had caught the dirty end of war's irony, had before that spent months, and in some cases years, in the demoralizing confines of prison camps, and yet were still soldiers. It was a thrilling sight to see this tatterdemalion column of men move smartly off at "quick march," erect, straight, and proud, arms swinging widely in the British fashion and heels pounding. Watching them, one could almost hear the skirl of pipes.

20

In the course of this move out of the fortress, I was guided down a different road just before our contingent reached the fenced compound where the Indians were taken. My place of confinement was to be a large old stone house on a hill that overlooked the compound but was about half a mile away. There I found four melancholy Italian officers, all in uniform. They were deserters who had skipped out of Italy equipped with baggage, and orderlies to carry it for them.

At this place I also found Gordon Fraser, an English bomber pilot who was as delighted as I was to have some Anglo-Saxon company at last. Thrown together as we were among this alien rabble of deserters, Gordon and I became fast friends, and I found the Englishman's friendship not only a relief from the company of these particular Italians, but a fine thing in itself. He was about my age, medium height, with straight brown hair, and possessed of a slightly foppish moustache. He looked every bit as English as he sounded, but like so many of the Royal Air Force fellows I had met, Gordon had a rollicking good sense of humor, and steel in his spine. His plane, a four-engine Lancaster bomber, had been shot down by German night-fighters on the return trip of a mission over Germany, and his crew bailed out over France. When I met him, he'd learned that two of his seven men, Canadians, had also made it to Switzerland.

Gordon and I speculated a bit about the attitude we should take toward the Italians who shared quarters with us. They were, after all, rather personable young men, and all officers. And in a sense we were all in the same boat, if for somewhat different reasons. But the idea of desertion was as abhorrent to Gordon as it was to me, and I could not deny a feeling of contempt for those men who walked out on their comrades when the going got rough. Worse, they strutted about quite brazenly in the uniforms they had disgraced. On the other hand, the more of these fellows who deserted, the fewer there would be for our men to fight. It occurred to me that I should recognize their service to our cause by being at least civil with them. So Gordon and I debated the problem, and by continuing to debate inconclusively we solved the problem by leaving the Italians pretty much alone.

One afternoon shortly after my arrival, Gordon roused me from a nap and asked me to come around to the back with him. He had found one of the Italian lads sitting on a stump crying and was afraid the fellow was hurt or sick. I thought it more likely that the man, in a fit of melancholy, was overcome by a sense of shame at having deserted. Or perhaps news of the savage war that was ravaging his homeland with increasing fury had saddened him to the point of tears.

We approached this handsome, husky young officer with real concern, and Gordon, whose French was very good, asked if he was ill. The fellow shook his head, turned his streaming face to the heavens, and moaned something in Italian. I then asked him what was the matter, prepared to hear him bewail the destruction of his home, or the loss of a member of his family. Instead, when he could restrain his unashamed weeping, the Italian told us he was overcome with sadness at being separated from his sweetheart in Milan, that it had been two weeks now, two long weeks since he had seen his beloved.

Mamma mia!

21

A Swiss officer came by our ramshackle villa a few days after our arrival and informed Gordon and me that we were shortly to be moved from there to a quarantine camp, where we would stay for a month—a very nice spa, he said, called Bad Lostorf—so the Swiss could be assured we brought no communicable diseases into their country. For a whole month! This was discouraging news, since we had been counting on an early beginning to the free and easy life of internment we had been hearing and speculating about.

One morning, after Gordon and I had been on the hill less than a week, we were marched off to the railroad station, baggage, Italians, and all. There we found the dozen or so assorted American and RAF crewmen, and all the Indians, who had been quartered in barracks in the compound; the whole lot of us were being taken to Bad Lostorf together. A few hours on the train, and then a walk through some lovely Swiss countryside up into swelling foothills, brought us to the spa, located just above a village.

In peacetime Bad Lostorf was, and probably is again, a resort hotel offering a clientele of modest circumstances baths in medicinal spring waters. One of the two main buildings contained twenty-five or so guest rooms, and in the basement rooms, carefully locked off from us, were the baths. The second building housed more guest rooms, two dining rooms, a lounge, and a little cafe with a terrace overlooking the valley.

The cafe was the one part of Bad Lostorf that kept up business as usual, while the rest of the spa, having been commandeered for service as the quarantine camp, was off limits to the natives. On Sundays quite a few villagers and people from the surrounding country came in to eat and drink on "our" terrace, and then the cafe was off limits to *us*, since we had not yet been decontaminated—of war fever, I guess. But the rest of the week, particularly in the evenings, those of us who had any money supplemented our diet of bread, cheese, and potatoes with coffee and cakes and, as often as possible, liquor.

The "camp" was run by a small detachment of Swiss soldiers under the direction of a Swiss first lieutenant, the commandant. This poor man had a nervous stomach and an obvious dislike of military duty, so the military control over us was very sketchy. The actual restraints put upon us there at Bad Lostorf were very few and were not vigorously enforced. We were supposed to be in our quarters by eleven o'clock at night, but when there was enough money among us for a lash-up in the cafe, we stayed up as long as the patron would serve us, which was usually until the money ran out. The limit to our wanderings away from the spa was also vague. If any of us had had any place he wanted to go, I suspect he could have simply walked out and wouldn't have been missed for days.

For amusement we had an assortment of indoor games like chess, checkers, and Monopoly. We could also listen in the cafe to the English language broadcasts of both the BBC and Germany's Axis Sally. Unfortunately we were not permitted to mail letters nor to send telegrams to our people, which many of us wanted to do.

Outdoors there was a makeshift volleyball court, and we Americans and British had some thunderous games against the highly competitive Indians. Both sides sustained so many injuries that we finally had to mix colors to keep East-West hostilities out of the competition. The Italians, now about a dozen in number, forever squabbling noisily among themselves, were considered beneath contempt by Indians and Anglo-Saxons alike, as much for the way they cheated one another out of their rations as for being deserters.

Our chief diversion was talk, however, and in the course of long bull sessions I learned the escape stories of some of the others. Tony Kosinsky, my roommate, was a stocky, round-faced lad from the stockyards area of Chicago, where his mother owned and operated a neighborhood grocery store. Tony's English was Southside Chicago, and when he had had a few drinks he was almost straight "dese" and "dose." One evening when a group of us were shooting the breeze, I got Tony's story. He was a P-47 pilot in an 8th Air Force fighter outfit, doing mainly bomber escort. He had mentioned once that he had bailed out of his plane, so I was a bit surprised when, after I had held forth on the delights of parachuting, he said wistfully, "I'd sure like to try that sometime!"

"It was this way," he explained. "We was coming back from escorting the heavies in to Friedrichshafen. We didn't meet any Jerries, so on the way back, after we left the big boys, the group commander was looking for something to shoot up on the ground. So we came to this big Kraut airfield just outside Dijon, and the CO calls out we'll go in and strafe, Lovejoy Squadron—that's us—first.

"We was at twenny thousand feet, and that fatheaded group CO circles us all the way down right over the goddam field! Jee*zus!* The time it takes us to ease down, they was able to bring in extra flak from the Russian front! I could see flares goin' off all over the place alerting the flak crews, and I begins to sweat.

"So we *finally* gets down and backs off for a pass, and in we go, me flying number two to the squadron CO. Just like I expected, dey trun up everything dey got, and blam! I catch one somewheres in my engine before I even fire my guns. They couldn't miss!

"Smoke begins pouring out and my engine gets rough— was I sweatin'! We get out of there fast, my CO coming in

close when I tell him I'm hit. My engine is getting rougher
and I can't get no altitude, so I decides to jump.

"I have one leg over the edge of the cockpit when the
engine begins to run a little smoother, and I think, She's
gonna be OK! So back in I get and try to get some altitude.
Then—rough again. I'm all set to pile out when she eases
up again. Jee*zus*! Then *whump!* No more engine! This time
I dive out and right away jerk the rip cord, because I know
I'm not very high up."

Beads of sweat stood out on Tony's balding pate, probably as much from the unaccustomed effort at describing as
from the recollection of those bad moments. "But," I said,
"then you *did* come down in a parachute."

"Ha!" he replied. "Fine ride! That damn parachute didn't
open until just a split second before I hit the ground!"

Tony was miles from the German airfield when he lit,
and Frenchmen got to him and took him in tow before the
Germans arrived on the scene. And luckily too, because he
had sprained an ankle on landing. Within a week or two the
French had smuggled him into Switzerland.

"Heyull, you fellers ain't heard *nothin'* yet!" This was
Tex Roskey, a wiry little staff sergeant bombardier with a
grin as wide as the state of Texas and a heart as big as the
sky above it. And, like the plains country he hailed from,
Tex was windy.

"I bet you I'm the *on'y* guy in this whole dayem club to
come down in a parachute headfirst. 'At's right. Head first,
by God! We got the heyull shot out of us over the target,
but were back over Belgium before number-two engine
commenced ta acting up. The pilot couldn't get the prop
feathered, and the first thing you know that whole plane
was ashakin' and abuckin' like a calf in a branding pen.
There I was trying to use the relief tube, jacket and pants
unfastened all the way down, and the chute harness
unbuckled, when the ruckshun commenced.

"I looked out the little ole winduh there to see what the
heyull was a-goin' on, and I swear that dayem wing was
flapping just like an old turkey buzzard. 'Tex,' I says to
myself, 'this big iron bird is ay-bout finished. Time you quit

workin' for Uncle Samuel and started workin' for yourself!' I was just fixin' to buckle myself together and make for the escape hatch when the panic bell went off. Well, sir, I got so excited I plumb forgot the bucklin' part and dove out the hatch right after the navigator.''

Tex ran a hand through his tawny mop, took a drink, and continued.

''Tumblin' around through the air there, all I could think was to pull the rip cord, and when that chute popped open it jerked me clean loose from my harness, all except for one leg. My chest buckle and one crotch strap was unbuckled, so the only part that was still hooked proper was that other crotch strap. So I come all the way down from fifteen thousand feet with just my one leg hooked through the harness, and landed on my head. Good thing too. I mighta sprained an ankle like Tony if I'd a come down feet first!''

I had run across Tex for the first time at our prequarantine collection compound where he was held with the other enlisted men, and he was giving the Swiss a bad time. They proposed to shave Tex's head, and he, in no uncertain terms, was having no part of it. As a hygienic precaution the Swiss required that soldiers seeking asylum in Switzerland have their heads shaved, but a number of the American and British crewmen objected. In an effort to get these mavericks in line, the officials had Gordon and me brought to the compound from our place on the hill. The exasperated Swiss officer in charge asked us to *order* the men to submit to the clippers. It didn't take me long to identify Tex as ringleader—and spokesman—of the resistance.

He was from Texas, by God, and no damn Sweitzer was a-goin' to shave *his* head, no sir, and the bastards could put him back across the border, but no clippers, no sir, by God! His chief cohort was a Canadian airman, one of Gordon's crew, and although the Canadian wasn't quite as eloquent as Tex, he was every bit as determined.

I told the Swiss officer that if he wanted a direct military order given these men, it would have to come from the American military attaché in Bern, that I had no authority over them. Furthermore, I wanted it understood that if he had any ideas about clipping *my* hair, forget it. Most of the men finally submitted to the Swiss officer's blustering, but Tex, the Canadian, and the two or three other bitter-enders were allowed to keep their hair. Not a one of the Indians was clipped, either, although as far as I know only the Sikhs had any valid plea, religious grounds, for leaving their hair intact.

Landing on his head had not addled Tex as much as it might have—"This here mesquite bush on my head cushioned the fall, sort of"—because he had wit enough to hide his chute and get himself out of sight right away. The Belgians got him soon after he landed and hid him and another fellow for several months in an outbuilding of a farm until they could be taken by the underground to Switzerland.

"Yes, sir," he continued, "every morning this sorry-looking old Belgique woman would come in, carry away the bucket we used for a toilet at night, and then bring it back full of boiled taters around noon. That old bucket sure did do double duty. Got us comin' and goin', ya might say."

Lieutenant Brown, pilot of a B-24 Liberator, was a college man, handsome, easygoing, and a bit vain about his lifeguard physique. His trouble, in common with a good many of us Americans, was that he just wasn't mad at anybody, even the Germans. The only people he even mildly disliked were the English.

When his plane packed up over Belgium on the way back from Germany, he ordered his crew to bail out. Being last out by a few minutes, he came down quite a ways from his men, and as he drifted down he saw that he would land a mile or so from a fairly large village. On the ground Brown thought things over, figured the odds were against him, and decided the hell with it, he would give himself up to the Germans. He was wearing a heavy, fleece-lined jacket over the regulation coverall-type flying suit, his overseas cap stuffed in the shin pocket on his right leg, and as usual had no Air Corps insignia showing on his flying garb. He walked to the village and started up the main street, his disgust at the unaccustomed walking, particularly on such a warm day, souring his expression and crowding out the uneasiness he otherwise would have felt. He walked toward a small group of German soldiers, but since they pointedly disregarded him, he ambled on past them, wondering just what a man had to do to give himself up.

When he was a dozen yards beyond the soldiers, Brown turned his head to see if they were beginning to show any interest in him, and he felt himself jostled. He whirled around and found he had brushed against another German, this one a noncommissioned officer. But this one simply glared at Brown a moment, then went on, muttering angrily. So Lieutenant Brown continued unhurriedly the entire length of this busy village street, attracting less attention than he would have garnered in an English village. At the far end of the village the street angled sharply and went on into the open country. Just around this bend Brown heard someone in a doorway say, "Pssssst—*Américain!*" and a hand beckoned him inside. From that point on he was in the hands of the Belgian underground. Evidently the German soldiers, and the villagers who saw him, had taken Brown for just another of the many Luftwaffe pilots walking home from an encounter with American or RAF fighters.

22

The talking, the volleyball, and the occasional drinking were all very fine, but these diversions spread pretty thin over the confinement and the monotony of bread, cheese and potatoes. Music and news from the BBC, and the excellent American dance music put out by Axis Sally, would have helped more, but the only radio we had access to was the one in the cafe. Breaks in the routine at Bad Lostorf were rare, so even the weekly bath and fumigating drill came as a welcome diversion. One day a week we were sprayed with a disinfectant and allowed a quick shower.

This bath deal was great so far as it went, but one bath a week in the summer simply was not enough. So my roommate's discovery, in the course of the second week, of a feasible entryway to the closed-off bath chamber in our building was a boon. Tony realized that the authorities would take a dim view of any uninvited use of their precious restorative waters, so he shared his secret only with me. Thereafter, until we were caught *in flagrante delicto* two weeks later, Tony and I had daily baths in our choice of the large tubs generously supplied with hot and cold water piped in from the springs. Discovery of our trespass was the occasion of one of my frequent official visits to the commandant's office.

We Americans were treated to the rumor, shortly after

we arrived at Bad Lostorf, that each man was entitled to an advance against his pay while in quarantine. A week passed and none of us in our crowd of new arrivals had received a cent, so except for a bit of change we could borrow from the earlier arrivals who had received advances, we were out of luck.

Then, unaccountably, Tex got a sizable payment of hard Swiss francs from Bern, and he set up drinks for the crowd that night. "When ole Tex has money, everybody has money!" he announced. It was quite a party, and as it gained momentum it sort of spread out. It seems that in the course of the outdoor phase of this wassail I caromed off a wall several times just under the commandant's window, so the next morning I was respectfully requested to present myself before The Man. His enumeration of my past infractions of the regulations, delivered laboriously in imperfect English, was lost in the buzzing in my aching skull. He finally pronounced sentence: I was to be restricted to my room for three days. He concluded, in his best officer-to-officer manner, that after I had served my penalty, "We could then continue as good friends, isn't it?" "Yes, sir," I replied, "it is."

I was in my second week at Bad Lostorf when the commandant informed me that I had been ordered to Bern for consultation—with the *Swiss* authorities, not the American! The American attaché had approved the interview, so I thought, what the hell, it'll be a change. I was sent off in the care of a taciturn Swiss soldier, and, after arriving in Bern, was escorted into the office of a smart-looking Swiss flying officer. What prompted this interview I never learned; I don't know who was supposed to "consult" whom about what. As it turned out, the Sweitzer did most of the talking, justifying at great length the Swiss Air Force case for having radio only in the flight commander's plane. The other three planes in the flight could be guided by the flight leader's hand signals!

After this pointless session, I presented myself at the American embassy, explained who I was, and requested some decent clothes and some money. I was still wearing

the rags I had came across the border in, so that reques
didn't need much pleading. I also allowed that I was hun
gry after my two weeks on quarantine rations. An Ameri
can officer from the attaché's office, dressed in civvies
took me in tow and got me outfitted fairly decently at a
secondhand-clothes shop, then took me to a restaurant and
told me to order up, that he would be back later to pay the
bill. I ordered a serving for two of roast beef with all the
trimmings, including a bottle of wine, and stowed it al
away. A pudding dessert followed by coffee and brandy
made me feel like a whole man again.

The bill was quite a surprise to the lieutenant, and
would like to believe that he paid it out of his own pocket.
had developed a distinct dislike for the fellow and for the
rest of the crowd in the attaché's office. They gave me the
impression that they considered escapees to be a lower
order of humans who, like indigent relatives, had to be
acknowledged but were best kept out of sight as much as
possible lest they be identified in the public mind with the
higher caste diplomatic corps Americans.

From the restaurant we went back to the lieutenant's
office, where I was given an advance on my pay, and then
was turned over to my Swiss soldier to be returned to Bad
Lostorf. There was rum for all hands that night, and once
again the welkin rang far into the wee hours. I awoke
shortly before noon the next day, fighting my way to con
sciousness through layers of misery and vague, uneasy
impressions about what had happened the night before.
recalled dimly that at one stage in the proceedings two of
us had plotted against the chastity of the squat young
barmaid in the cafe, but I couldn't recall what we had done
about it. Reluctantly I put my body together and got dressed
determined to learn the worst. I was also curious to find
out why I had not long since been summoned to the
commandant's office.

I met Tony in the hall, and he assured me that nothing o
any importance had happened in Bad Lostorf during the
night. But plenty had happened a couple of hundred mile
to the west of us, on the Normandy beaches. It was June 6

and by the time I came fully awake the Allied forces were firmly ashore in France. The BBC had crackled the news around the world like a gigantic electric shock, and it brought us in Bad Lostorf alive with excitement. Small wonder that the commandant, being a prudent sort, had chosen to ignore the relatively less damaging American action in his own theater during the night.

It was on this day, June 6, that my wife and parents were informed by the War Department that I was safe in Switzerland.

23

The month at Bad Lostorf finally ended, and our crowd
was again shepherded through the lovely countryside and
entrained, this time for the bright lights of Bern. That city,
which we were able to see something of in our four days
there, exceeded my fondest expectations with its blend of
the very old and the surprisingly modern. Best of all, it was
lighted at night, and after spending nearly two years with
England's blackout it was wonderful to see streetlights and
neon signs and lighted store windows again. Another thing
I liked about Bern was the almost total absence of uniforms.
Girls in bright dresses, cycling through the streets, their
skirts billowing and revealing clean, tanned legs, were an
eye-catching sight. After the grim drabness of England at
war, this Swiss city was a fairyland of color and sound.

In Bern we were told that the town of Glion, down on
Lake Geneva, was the place where we, along with other
American and British air forces escapees, were to spend
the rest of the war. Checking a map, Tony and I found that
Glion was a village near Montreux, a town situated at the
eastern end of Lake Geneva's north shore. The village
seemed to be back quite a ways from the lake. We were
also told that we would live in resort hotels, not the best,
but adequate, and that we would be paid on the first of
each month. We would have absolutely no military or any

other duties to perform and would wear civilian clothes.

This all sounded fine to me. I had a long list of books in mind that I could, at last, begin to read. And I could study French at the Berlitz School in Montreux, and perhaps German too, in preparation for the Ph.D. I hoped to take after the war. I had always nursed a vague yearning to become a scholar, a widely read man of letters. The prospect of weeks or possibly months of leisure on the summer shores of Lake Geneva revived my aspirations to intellectual betterment.

When our train arrived at Montreux, we transferred immediately to a cogwheel train, which clanked off into the mountains. We soon learned that Glion is not just inland from Montreux, as it appeared on the map, it is also quite a bit above. Its full name is Glion sur Montreux, and it seemed that from anyplace in the village you could throw a rock into the town below.

The village is situated on a sort of shelf in the side of a mountain that towers steeply on up to join its gigantic brethren in somber majesty behind. Glion is mostly hotels, but there are quite a number of houses packed neatly among them. The cobbled streets go from level to level the best way they can, and it is all very quaint.

The hotel I was assigned to was a modest three-story building whose second floor opened onto the main street, which wound up from the train station to the larger hotels farther uphill. Though it was not so modern a place as the hotel occupied by the larger body of Americans, the Hotel Glion had much the better view. The side away from the street faced the south, looking out over the lake. From the little terrace behind and off the first floor of our hotel, a grassy yard in peacetime but planted now with potatoes, the mountain descended steeply to Montreux, on the little plain along the lake.

I could stand on the balcony outside my window and see the winding of the road down the mountainside to the lakeshore below; and moored close to the shore just to the east was the Chateau de Chillon, looking like a bit of arrested antiquity. The mountains were sharp and steep on

the other side of the lake, and down at the end of the lake
the Rhone Valley, flat between two ranges of mountains,
swept off to the east. In the distance could be seen th
Dents du Midi, a high snow-capped mountain range tha
dominates the valley.

Tony Kosinsky and I, again sharing a room, settled ou
few belongings in place very quickly and wandered aroun
talking with the other fellows: Brown, who had left Ba
Lostorf a couple of weeks earlier and was there in the roon
next to ours, Tex, Walt Wiggins, several others I knew
and maybe a dozen others I didn't know. We met Kitty
the middle-aged English woman who managed the hotel fo
the young Swiss fellow who owned the place and double
as chef. Kitty was very indulgent and patient in the face o
what seemed to me pretty outrageous behavior on our part
She had one glass eye, so maybe she didn't see all tha
went on.

In the middle of the afternoon I got word to go to th
other hotel to see Doug Hovecamp, the ranking officer and
therefore commanding officer of the American group. H
towered over me as we shook hands, then settled his lank
form in a chair as he introduced me to the two othe
officers in the room. After some rambling conversation
Doug observed that I had a very low serial number an
looked at me expectantly. I guess it did seem strange that
was still only a first lieutenant when most fellows with my
time in the service were captains and majors.

So I explained that our air group had been shipped t
England in October of 1942 as part of the "two thousan
aircraft" that President Roosevelt reportedly had been will
ing to sacrifice in an abortive landing on the French coas
to relieve the pressure on the Russians at Stalingrad. Bu
since Churchill stood firm against such a wasteful project
our outfit sat around England for nearly sixteen month
doing nothing but flying around over the country in battle
weary Spitfires. No mortality, so no turnover, so n
promotion.

"Were you really captured by the Germans?" Hovecamp
asked. I had noticed a trick he had of turning his face i

profile to a person who was speaking to him and gazing fixedly at nothing. Perhaps it was more of a mannerism than a trick, but the way he did it seemed to apply an automatic discount to whatever might be said in response. He had a strikingly good profile, with a well-shaped, carefully barbered head. When I said yes, I had been a prisoner but had escaped, it didn't sound true even to me.

"Since you are ranking man at the Glion, I guess you are elected to be in charge," he continued after a pause. "You won't have much to do, just keep track of your fellows and help keep them out of trouble." He paused a moment, then went on.

"We don't have any rules, or very many, anyway. For the sake of appearances, we require everyone to wear a coat or jacket in the dining room for lunch and dinner. And everyone has to be off the streets of Montreux by midnight. Everything's closed down there by then anyway, so that's no strain.

"There's one problem the manager of the Glion is complaining about, though, that you might be able to help us with," he continued. "One of the men has got a girl staying with him, and the owner thinks he ought to be paying room rent for her. It didn't make much difference at first, when there were only a few of our fellows there, but now he's afraid that all you guys are going to park women on him. You might talk to your guy, get him to put his girl in a separate room or something."

Hovecamp saw the puzzlement on my face and added, "Pierre doesn't mind women in the hotel, you understand, he only objects to having them move in sort of permanently without paying." Another pause. "Just explain to the new fellows that they have to pay for anything they break. Actually, you guys are lucky, you have that basement room for your riots. And you can trust Kitty, she won't overcharge you for what you drink."

24

As I walked back to the Glion, I felt just a little bit of annoyance at the notion Hovecamp had given me that things were likely to be noisy around our hotel. But then, I thought, I can do my reading during the day and go walking, or go to the library or to a movie in town during the evening. My ivory tower restored to view, I felt better. But first, of course, we ought to crank up a party to celebrate our liberation from Bad Lostorf. I quickened my pace, thinking of the crisp franc notes in my pocket.

Dinner was at six, and it was wonderful. I ate like a starved man. I thought a bottle of wine out on the terrace would round off the meal and ease me into a properly reflective mood to plan my activities for the next day. I should have known better. Halfway through the bottle of wine I felt the familiar tuning-up of excitement in me. The sky was clear and the end of the day was still with us, and there was laughing to do and wine to be drunk and women to be seen.

"Brown," I called, "how do we get down off this alp to where there are people and these nightclubs you were telling us about?"

"Spoken like a true man," he answered. "We go by the funic, then walk to the nearest bistro. From there we work our way to the *Perroquet*, and keep your hands off my two-tone blond!''

"What is this perrokay where we find the blond?" I asked.

"That," said he, "is our only real, high-class nightclub. You can just sign a chit for your drinks there, these fools trust you! But we're wasting time, men. Advance! *En voiture pour* Montreux!"

Tony found himself swept up in an enthusiasm he shared only slightly. Tex came clattering down the stairs calling, "You dayem fools aimin' to go out on a drunk without ole Tex along to pertek ya? Come on, Walt, the Sweitzers is gonna catch it tonight!" Brown led the way to the funicular station, where we bought tickets and piled aboard.

There were four ways of getting from Glion to Montreux, roughly a mile off as the crow files. These were the funicular, the cogwheel train, the highway (via taxi), and a pathway. The simplest, quickest, and cheapest was the funicular, a contraption consisting of parallel rails running in a steep, straight line from top to bottom. One small rail coach ran on each track, and the two cars were connected by a cable that looped over a pulley at the top station. The cable was just long enough so that when one car was at the top station, the other was at the bottom. The power employed was simple gravity. The car at the top took on an enormous quantity of water in tanks built for the purpose, and at a signal, the conductors on both cars released their brakes and the load of water pushed the high car down, pulling the other one up. Once at the bottom, the ladened car disgorged its water with a sound like the Jolly Green Giant pissing, and the other car took on its load from the high station.

This dinky rig ran from a station on the east edge of Montreux straight up to Glion, just a block from our hotel. And although we heathens tended to look upon the whole affair as a rustic joke, the functionaries who ran the trains were quite serious about their responsibilities. In all the many times I rode the funic, I never detected a hairsbreadth of variance in the routine. The conductor would admit his passengers, collect the tickets, and then, with an exchange of warning signals, would call out, *"En voiture!"* Occasionally there would be a way-stop at one of the two or three places along the route where people were allowed to disembark for the villas scattered up and down the slope, and in each such case the conductor would call out the name of the stop. Invariably he also announced the terminal station as though conveying surprising news to the passengers; as though they might conceivably have wound up at Caux, far on up the mountain, or perhaps at Bern.

After I had ridden the funic about fifty times, I suggested to one of the conductors as we traveled up from Montreux one day that when we got up to the top he should announce Les Avants instead of Glion. He looked at me as though I were crazy and stated, *"Mais c'est impossible, monsieur! We go only as far as Glion!"*

The mode of transportation to Montreux favored next to the funic was the cogwheel train, which toiled up a formidable grade from Montreux through Glion to Caux and points beyond. It was a much more conventional and serious undertaking than the funic, and although its bottom terminus was closer to the heart of town, it was more expensive and ran less frequently.

The third mode, employed almost exclusively by Americans, was Glion's one-man, one-car taxi company. It was one of the few privately owned automobiles I saw in Switzerland that burned gasoline, a rare commodity in wartime. Most automobiles, and they were few enough, had converter devices on them that made low-order combustibles out of all sorts of fuel bases. This taxi was also available, always, at any hour of the day or night. And, as we were to learn, it was available for use beyond the ordinary confines of the law.

The most remarkable feature about this taxi was its driver. He was an angular individual of about thirty-five with an air of courteous independence, which of itself distinguished him from the more obsequious breed of tourist caterers about him. He was also lacking in that prudent conservatism associated with the sober, industrious Swiss. He drove

that black sedan like a man possessed, oblivious of fuel and
tire shortages, heedless of life and limb.

But it was fun seeing and hearing him perform. From a
number of places in Montreux it was possible to look up at
the side of the mountain below Glion and trace, at night,
the tortuous path of the road by the headlights of the
madman's taxi. And in the quiet of the small hours one
could hear clearly the screeching of tires on the horseshoe
bends, because this man seemed to think it was necessary
in his line of duty to reduce speed only slightly, if at all,
when taking corners. He was the one relief in the solid
Swiss phalanx of caution, industry, and meticulous, law-
abiding orderliness among the natives of Glion.

Used only in extremis, or by those who succumbed to
misbegotten physical culture notions, was the fourth route
to town: a steep, partially stepped pathway, which began
its descent fifty yards down the road from our hotel and
negotiated a close to forty-five-degree slope. It was suitable
for donkeys and fanatics, too tough a course, given its
steep grade and sharp switchbacks, for a casual stroller. I
made an acquaintance with this trail by traveling down it
the first time against my will long past midnight. I walked
the trail the second time only to see just how close I had
come to breaking my fool neck the night before.

Our crowd, led by Brown, left the lower funic station
and headed for town. It was a pleasant walk from the
station into Montreux, through a little park, past some
residences, and then into the shop district. Our first stop
was a sidewalk cafe across the street from, of all things, a
soda fountain. At this bistro we sat under a superb evening
sky and drank Specials, a concoction made of port wine
and brandy. It tasted good, and seemed to give body to my
anticipation of an exciting evening. Life was fine, these
were fine fellows to be with, full of wit and laughter, and
the evening was pregnant with adventure.

"I feel like climbing that there mountain, boys. That one
there, with the sunlight on top. It looks real purty."

"Waste of time, Tex," Brown replied. "You'd do better
trying to climb the waitress over there in the soda joint."

"That there's the mountain I'm a-talkin' about, that chesty blond. Let's get on to this perrukay place, Brown, this soda pop is about to put me to sleep."

"Easy, boy," Brown replied, "the joint doesn't open until nine and we've got one more stop to make first. Let's go!"

We walked on through Montreux to the west side, down to the edge of the lake, where Brown steered us to a place called Pavillon des Sports. A dance hall where you could also drink wine and eat, the Pavillon had a fine terrace dance floor out on the lakeside as well as the main ballroom inside. This was about the only place, we learned, where it was possible to meet girls from town. They went there stag, much as the girls at home would go to the dance places at the lake resorts. We had a fine time there for two hours that first evening, drinking wine on the terrace and dancing with the girls, some of whom were pretty but who would not come to our table and join in the wine drinking. One girl told me that it would ruin a girl's reputation to be seen going about, or even drinking wine at a table, with an American. But we didn't mind. We drank a lot of wine, which was cheap and good, and we talked and laughed a great deal.

After a while we left the Pavillon and walked back to the Perroquet, a ritzy little nightclub on the second floor of a building in the downtown district. Only one section of the place was open, however, because with the war on, the club didn't have much trade. The music was provided by a man who played drums and guitar and sang, very low-key and conventional. He was a huge black man in a white suit. It seemed strange to us to hear this man speak and sing French, and to see him walking around the town during the day with his very blond, lovely wife.

There wasn't much doing at the Perroquet, so we had a bottle of wine, danced with the two hostesses there, then headed back to the hotel. We had missed the last funic for the night, so Brown called the taxi, and we whooped as we stood in the quiet street and saw his headlights negotiating the switchback road. Full of wine, we enjoyed the excitement of that mad ride back up the mountain.

Back at our hotel we could hear a party in full swing in the basement room. I went up to my room to leave my jacket before joining the brawl and stepped out on the balcony for a look at the lake by starlight. But as my eyes became accustomed to the dark I noticed someone else out there, and the man cleared his throat just as I realized this guy was all tangled up with a girl. I had a glimpse of the ice bucket with a magnum sticking out of it as I turned back to my room.

"I guess I should have warned you," Brown explained downstairs. "Sometimes the girls are a little reluctant to drink in our rooms, so we use your porch there for special dates. You'd be surprised what an impression it makes on a girl, sitting out there under the stars with Kitty serving champagne."

The party downstairs had hit the singing stage. Tony Ornatek, also from Chicago, played his guitar, and we sang ribald songs. Tony didn't play very well, but that made no difference. Somebody threw an empty bottle through the open window, and Tex yelled, "Don't do that. Jack has a girl out there in the tater patch. You could kill a man with a heavy bottle like that."

"What a wonderful way to die!"

"Ain't nobody out there now. I was just out to take a leak, and saw Jack chasing his broad around the corner."

"Jeezus! Those spuds will make fine eating by the time you drunken bastards get through hosing them down every night. *Pommes de terre à la pissoire.*"

"Ought to make Tex feel right at home."

"Like heyull!" yelled Tex. "I done had enough *pissoire* potatoes in Belgium. The next sonofabitch I see takin' a leak in the tater patch, I'm a-goin' to knock him clean offa this here mountain."

"Give him enough warning so's he can get his pants buttoned up, Tex. Don't want a guy standing in the middle of Montreux with his fly open. Wouldn't be safe."

Tony struck up with,

  "Standin' on a corner, standin like a man,
    Standin' on a corner with a buck in my han'.
    Cigar butts, orange peels, candy wrappers—"

Somebody yelled, "Play 'Mary Ann McCarthy,' Tony." Tony struck a chord, and half a dozen voices joined in to the tune of the "Battle Hymn of the Republic." A guitar string broke with a loud ping. Tony looked at the guitar a moment, then slammed it flat to the floor, climbed onto his chair, and jumped, his feet aimed at the instrument. I snatched the guitar away just in time, and Tony glared at me accusingly.

"Tony, you crazy bastard," said Brown, "that's the third guitar you've bought in two weeks. Just go put another string on it, don't smash it."

"Bill has a broad upstairs, use the elastic out of her drawers for a string. From what I hear, that ought to make real good music."

Tony took the guitar from me and weaved out of the room.

"Kitty, more wine! Here, Hickman, that glass is dirty, let me get you a fresh one." Wiggins, bleary-eyed and grinning, took my glass and threw it in the corner. A dozen other glasses followed it, and to the tinkle of the smashing wine glasses was added the heavier crash of an empty bottle.

Kosinsky walked in the door from outside, his balding head glistening with perspiration and his round face all smiles. "No more music tonight, boys! Ornatek just threw his guitar outta his window. Damn if it didn't play a chord from 'Mary Ann McCarthy' when it hit, too!"

25

The next day I woke just before ten and had Kitty bring me a breakfast of coffee, toast, and jam in bed. I then joined Tony and Brown out on the balcony, where we three tried to bake the misery out of us. As the warm sun eased the pounding in my head, I reminded myself to begin my morning walks tomorrow for sure. After lunch I soothed my conscience by going to the library in Montreux. There I selected two books, *Back to Methuselah,* by Shaw, and the other an endless tale about Vidal, the French troubadour of the late Middle Ages. This was a promising beginning to my lofty project for intellectual betterment. Unfortunately, it was also the ending. Those were the only two books I read the whole time I was in Switzerland.

During the first week in Glion, I was eager to explore all the different things there were to do. There was swimming in the afternoon, either down the lakeshore at Territet, where there was all sorts of beach equipment, or right in Montreux, where the facilities were less elaborate but adequate. The sights at both places were rewarding. The Swiss girls took two bathing suits to the beach, one serviceable and well-worn for actual swimming, and one fancy one, usually very scanty, for lying in the sun. Those Swiss gals were athletic, and their exertions certainly didn't hurt their figures. After swimming there was the pleasure of a restorative after-swim drink, quaffed at a table in a sidewalk cafe, or at the Pavillon. Dinner always tasted fine after such an afternoon, either at one of the restaurants in town or back at the hotel, where the meals were always good. In the evening there was dancing, drinking, an occasional movie, or a combination of the three.

The 150 Americans and perhaps twice that number of British Royal Air Force people in Glion, augmented by the uncounted hundreds of British Army internees up at Caux, guaranteed a rich variety of excitement around Montreux. I suppose if there had been only a handful of internees there, life would have become a fairly steady, quiet thing for us. There were enough of us, however, that we created our own freewheeling, often inane, always noisy society.

The Swiss, of course, were frequently the butt of our jokes, but only because they happened to be the natives. None of us felt hostile toward them, but neither could we warm up to them. We were simply a troop of young men abruptly removed from the demanding discipline and daily uncertainties of combat and dumped into a life of undisciplined leisure. Although my conscience bothered me some at first, I very soon acknowledged that Glion was not, as I had thought at first glance, an ivory tower. It was bedlam, and I had best relax and enjoy it.

We were quietly oiling the wheels of pandemonium one afternoon when Kitty called me from the terrace with the news that there was a Swiss soldier in the foyer who wished to speak with the commandant. I formed up and marched into the foyer with as much authority as I could muster on short notice and found that there was indeed a soldier there. Or half a one, anyway. He was under five feet tall, and when he stood at attention to salute with his rifle ordered, he and his gun were almost of a length. He was in full gear, from oversized field uniform to the ridiculous canopied helmet.

In very good English, the corporal explained that he was here to conduct one Lt. Donald Toye to prison for a series of specified instances of misconduct while he was being processed through Bern two or three weeks earlier. The charges, as I recall, included violating the curfew; creating a disturbance in a bar; defying and evading a police officer who tried to arrest him; and finally, when he was taken, falsifying his name. He was to be taken to jail for ten days, and the corporal showed me the orders, properly endorsed by the American authorities. We all understood what jail in Switzerland meant: a bread-and-water diet, and no tobacco.

Toye was a tall, easygoing, and extremely likable fellow, but with such an air of studied correctness about him that the charges were rather surprising. He was not at the hotel just then, so pending his return I invited the little corporal to have a drink with us. I then hallooed up the gang and told them what was afoot. In the course of our wait, while we plied the soldier with wine, I commented on the rubber nib covering the mouth of the rifle barrel, asking if he removed it before firing. He seemed astonished at the notion of firing the rifle, so I asked him what he would do if his prisoner tried to escape. Would he shoot? The prospective prisoner, I added, was a pretty big man. The corporal said of course he would not shoot under any circumstances. If he did, he would have to clean the rifle barrel, which the Swiss military insisted be kept perfectly clean at all times.

When Toye arrived, the party was roaring along on a high note of expectancy. I told him he was under arrest and should pack for his stay as a guest of the Swiss government. His only comment was that he guessed he would finally get to read that book he had been working on for a week, and upstairs he went. At his reappearance we played a record of Jelly Roll Morton's musical account of a Dixieland funeral. It starts out with a wailing discordant sound, and then a solemn voice intones, "Ashes to ashes, and dust to dust! If the women don' get ya, the liquor must!" More wailing, a brisk drum roll-off, and into a hot jazzy chorus.

The corporal looked distressed at all this hilarity, but his special disapproval was reserved for the escort he got to the funic station. Perhaps he had expected trouble; he was, after all, a soldier sent out to arrest an officer of a foreign power and take him to jail. I am certain that the last thing he expected was the bibulous foofaraw we made of the whole proceeding.

He acquitted himself very well, but the whole situation was so apt and obvious a caricature of two nationalities that it was very funny. The baggy-suited, earnest little soldier with the rubber-capped rifle was Switzerland personified, and the tall, amiable, good-looking Toye was as American as a square dance. The nature of the charges, the reaction of the prisoner to the charges, and the whooping "funeral" procession to the funic station gave substance to the caricature. When Toye returned ten days later, not much the worse for wear, he told us that the little corporal had tried during the entire trip to get from him a sensible understanding of what all the hilarity had been about.

26

Switzerland during the war was a haven for all sorts of people anxious to get out of the way of trouble. Vevey provided sanctuary for a large group of Jews from Holland who had only just managed to get to safety from Hitler's hideous pogrom. There were also a number of very wealthy people—Poles, Italians, and Greeks, among others—who got to Switzerland with enough treasure to ride out the war in comfort and style. This group, relatively few in number, occupied the more expensive hotels in Glion and Montreux. They were mostly the remnants of what had been a glittering international set that moved in a splendid migration from one European resort to another. I'd read about these people but had never expected to see any of them up close.

The tea at Mrs. Thurston's villa, however, did give me an opportunity to rub elbows with some of this crowd. This lady, an American of the international breed who was caught in Switzerland by the war and compelled to stay on, gave a tea periodically for the purpose of acquainting ''some of the nicer American officers'' (and being officers, presumably gentlemen) with some of the better people about.

I went to the tea under the misapprehension that it was to be a cocktail party, but after one circuit of the grounds I decided to stay on in spite of my dislike for Mrs. Thurston and tea. For there I met a countess with an unpronounceable Polish name, an American-born beauty of about thirty who was waiting with less and less hope for word from her husband, an officer in the Polish army. There I also met the one resident count (not connected with the one resident countess), one of the ragtag of international nobility who carried his years well, made his living by treating with elegant courtliness those women who could afford his special attentions, and who irritated me with his cynicism. And, lastly, there was an exquisitely beautiful young Greek girl.

This girl was not only breathtakingly beautiful, she spoke perfect American English. I made a date with her and the next afternoon presented myself at her hotel. One of those ugly, ornate monuments to the dead age of lavish migrations, it was now practically empty. I was led through one huge deserted salon after another, footsteps lost in thick carpeting until we came to a balcony terrace overlooking the lake. There I waited while the man fetched the girl.

She drank tea, and I drank wine while I listened to this wonderful creature talk. She had learned English mostly from listening to American phonograph records, for which she had that peculiar European passion. She had been out of Greece only twice in her life, and when the war threatened the family had moved to Switzerland to wait out the war.

Whether from our present surroundings or from what she said, I gained the impression of overpowering wealth and tradition in this girl's life. She was from a world as far removed as Mars from the world I knew. But for all the evident wealth and ease of her life, she was unaffected and sweet. And I had to keep reminding myself that this poised sleek creature was only sixteen, since she had the assured manner of a woman twice her age. Which is probably the reason I never went to see her again. She, with a hundred generations looking over her shoulder, lived at a measured cadence that would take her only as far in a year as I was accustomed to covering in a day.

The countess, whom I visited a number of times, since she stayed at one of the big hotels in Glion, was older, and being American, more comprehensible to me. But she too gave me the impression of barely perceptible movement. An afternoon with her meant walks in the garden, tea on the terrace, or tea in the salon against the backdrop of a scattered score of murmuring ancients and a chamber group of genteel musicians playing string music. On the real jazzy days there would be a daring glass of sherry. Such "events" were certainly restful, and conversation with this woman gave me glimpses of an undreamed-of existence. But I was not designed for the minuet.

27

Our Allied community provided a setting where you could wake up in the morning and feel reasonably certain that something unusual would happen before you went to bed that night. Like the time I fell off, or nearly fell off, our alp.

It was a placid afternoon when Walt Wiggins and I got slicked up and headed to Montreux to meet our dates. Walt's date was an American girl named Elaine who lived in Vevey with her mother and her Swiss stepfather, and my date was a friend of Elaine's, whom I met that day for the first time, a hefty Swiss girl named Denise. She was a member of the Swiss army WAC.

Elaine, the American, knew a great many people in Montreux, so we spent a pleasant afternoon drinking wine at a succession of bistros along the lake, and we ended the rounds with a wonderful fondue dinner. Eating fondue in the Swiss manner is enhanced by a rule that whoever loses a piece of bread in the cheese is required to kiss all members of the opposite sex at the table. A fondue dinner is also helped by the other rule, which prohibits the drinking of water during, and for one hour after, the meal. Wine must be drunk instead.

After dinner, some spirit moved us to go up to Glion to the fancy big hotel, where there was a snappy bar on the order of an American taproom. A brief shower of rain caught us on the way up on the funic, and at Elaine's suggestion we took off our shoes and proceeded barefoot to the hotel. Since we would probably be the only guests in the taproom, we didn't think our bare feet would cause any raised eyebrows.

But we weren't the only ones there. A party of eight or ten British officers had come down from Caux, and they were enjoying the company of one brassy blond woman. It was obvious that a ball was in the making, but since we didn't know any of the Britishers, we had a bottle of wine and left, the evening still young. Walt and I saw the girls to the cogwheel train, and he decided to call it a day. I was still curious about that party, and had also concluded that the waiter had gypped me, so I went back to the bar.

With a little persuasion, the waiter saw it my way, and I was sitting with my drink at a ringside seat when things seemed to explode on the British side of the room. I learned later that as the party began to pick up momentum, the waiter who had given me a bad time undertook to quiet the Britishers. His latest effort in that direction set off the explosion. One of the revelers grabbed the waiter by the lapels, hustled him to the bar, then pitched him over and told him to bloody well stay there.

It was then I noticed that all the men were barefooted. They'd liked the idea when they saw our party earlier and had followed suit. The waiter disposed of, a game of follow-the-leader began, and their party, increased by now to about twenty, swept me up in the game. This was followed by singing, a rough game of rugby, and an indistinct blur of assorted frenetic activities.

It was past midnight when I found myself, steadied by the brisk night air and with my shoes on my feet, walking down the street in the direction of my hotel between two strapping men from the party. South Africans they were, and like all the South African officers I ever saw, both were well over six feet tall and solid in the shoulders.

They were on the way to Montreux, they told me, and I must go along. But I was done in, and respectfully declined their invitation. When we came abreast of my hotel door I said good night and made to turn away. But these amiable brutes, one on each side, simply lifted me off the ground and carried me along, protesting, the fifty yards to where that damnable footpath to Montreux began. The funic and the cogwheel, of course, had long since quit for the night.

So down we went, one of the giants ahead of me and one behind, and none of us in fit shape to navigate a straight road, let alone this trail. The first two or three stretches were faintly illuminated by the streetlight at the beginning of the trail, but after that it was pitch-dark. Neil, the leader, produced a box of matches, and by those intermittent sparks of light we rattled our hilarious, death-defying course toward Montreux. Finally Neil was out of matches, so he called back to Harry, twenty yards to the rear. There was a pause, and Harry announced he had some matches. He struck one, missed his step, and came bouncing down a series of crude steps on his rear, the match, held aloft, lighting the amazed look on his face.

Neil and I whooped with laughter at this prize vision, and it was a little while before we got under way again. A bit later I missed my step at one of the switchbacks, one of the few where the trouble had been taken to make a sort of square landing of cement. As I lost my balance, I managed to twist around and catch the edge of the landing with my hands, and there I hung along a sheer cliff, which for all I knew might have been fifty feet down. I yelled for the others, and they finally located me, but were laughing so hard they didn't think to heave me up. The two crouched there above me, a match held out over the chasm, pointing at me and shouting with laughter.

They finally hauled me up when it appeared I couldn't hang on much longer, and we went on our way. By the time we got to Montreux the wine had worn off and I was completely done in, so I telephoned the Glion cabbie and rode back to my hotel. The next morning I began to worry about what *might* have happened to me. I walked down the trail before lunch and found the spot where I had hung. It was a sheer drop of some thirty feet from that landing before the ground sloped out a bit to some trees.

Whatever it was we did, however, and wherever we went, there was always an awareness of the lake—its presence dominated the place. Lake Geneva was a thing of startling moods: molten under the lowering of a summer storm; sparkling gaily blue, incredibly blue, in the morning sun; serene and darkly silver by moonlight. Someone had told me that the earliest villages of primitive man in these parts were built on stilts over the water at the extreme eastern end of the lake, in a little backwater cove just north of where the Rhone River barges in. One day when we were sailing I was shown pilings, the tops a foot or so beneath the surface, which were said to be the remnants of one of these early villages. Whether these actually were remains of such early habitations I don't know, but it impressed me to be near a spot, so close physically but so remote in years, where earliest man, Swiss edition, was supposed to have lived.

One night very late, after an evening of mild carousing, I wandered alone down to the water's edge, too restless to go back up to the hotel with the others. The city was dead asleep, and the only sounds I heard as I stared out over the water were those of the water hens, calling and sputtering as they sailed along in the mist.

I must have dozed off after a while, because I became aware, with a startling suddenness, that I was cold and cramped. But another sensation made me forget my discomfort and brought me wide-awake. I felt as though time had come unstuck at the nether end and I had slid back to a time of no-man, back into an age that belonged solely to the mountains and the eerie cries of the waterfowl. In one hushed moment, I saw that lake ten thousand years ago, a mist making it steam gently in the moon's unnatural light. It was a place without a name in a valley without bearing and outside the knowledge of yet nonexistent mankind. It was there, being seen by man for the first time at this moment. I was almost surprised when I roused myself and looked around to find the buildings of Montreux slumbering behind me.

28

It was in Switzerland I came the closest I was to come in the whole war to getting a Purple Heart awarded to me. And it was only by some furious backpedaling on my part, and by the effective intercession of a friend at our embassy in Bern, that I was able to avoid the honor.

I was injured, right enough, but it wasn't an injury incurred in line of duty, at least not *combat* duty, and I sure didn't want the attention of my wife, nor of the progeny I was certain would appear on the scene in due course, called to it in later years.

What happened was that Denise, the leggy Swiss WAC, nearly broke my arm. Or rather it's what she did to me that caused *me* to nearly break my arm. It was on my second or third date with her, again in company with Walt and Elaine, and we were sitting at a bistro table in Montreux when I began to think Denise was indeed a very good idea. She was about my height and, though a bit robust for my taste, had sparkle and a lively sense of humor.

As afternoon waned I suggested we all go back up to the hotel for dinner, and the girls agreed readily enough. After dinner we had some more wine out on the balcony as evening faded into night at about the same pace as my ardor grew to full stature. A bit of necking convinced me that all systems were go—Denise appeared to be as eager as I was.

She agreed to go to my room, where I said I would show her the little Baretta pistol I had acquired, but when I glanced around from rummaging in my dresser drawers for the damned thing, I saw she had shucked off all her clothes but her skimpy panties. In the time it took her to get those off, I got myself secured for battle action, Denise protesting as she climbed into bed that she wasn't *that* kind of a girl.

In those days I wasn't very prudent, so I piled in on top of her magnificent body, found the shank, and thrust my spur in deep. She matched my thrust with a buck that threw me over, clean out of the bed, and in the fall I whacked my left arm on the nightstand by the bed.

My arm hurt, but what the hell! I quickly remounted, but was careful to stirrup my toes in the ironwork at the foot of the bed. It was the wildest ride of my career up to that point, but I made the whole course without further trouble, my sore arm forgotten.

The next morning my arm hurt so bad I thought the bones must be cracked, so I carried it in a sling made for me by Kitty. All would have been well, and my arm would have healed with no fuss (as it did in a week or so) except that this was the day our military attaché, General Legge, and his wife were to visit Glion, to be feted at an afternoon tea dance. And it was a command performance; all hands were to be present, and all officers were carefully instructed to dance with the matronly Mrs. Legge.

When my turn came, Mrs. Legge asked me what was wrong with my arm, and I said very casually it was nothing but a minor combat injury and was already nearly healed.

"Oh," she said, "you're that Lieutenant Hickman who escaped from the Germans, aren't you?"

I admitted with becoming modesty that I was, and at that point was relieved when one of the other men cut in. I thought that was that, until word filtered back that General Legge planned to have me decorated with a Purple Heart. I hadn't known he was medal-happy—he himself was reputed to be the most decorated general in the American army at the start of World War II—and it had never occurred to me that Mrs. Legge would call his attention to my "combat" injury.

Katy bar the goddam door! I telephoned Sgt. Joe Coss at the attaché office and asked him what was up. He confirmed the worst, and I told him he just had to come down to Glion and talk to me. He liked an excuse to get out of Bern, so down he came. I gave him all the details, and he admitted it could become a very sticky wicket indeed, especially for me. He had some fun at my expense making up wording for the special orders that would go with the award.

But somehow Joe got the machinery stopped, and I never heard another word about a Purple Heart. How many times since have I had reason to be thankful to Joe! There's a scenario that later used to run through my mind:

Son Stevie, aged four: "Daddy, tell us about the war."

Son Lance, aged three: "Tell us about how you were wounded."

Son Stevie: "Yes, Mommy showed us your Distinguished Flying Cross and your Air Medal and your Purple Heart."

Son Lance: "Did it hurt much, Daddy? Show us your scar."

Of such stuff are nightmares made!

29

As the Fourth of July approached, we at the Hotel Glion were surprised to learn that fireworks would be on sale in Montreux. In honor of the day, and because we had been paid just the day before, we decided that a celebration was in order. With all twenty-eight of us contributing, we figured on quite a pyrotechnic display that evening. Pierre, the manager of the hotel, entered into the spirit of things by putting a small American flag at each place for lunch, and by preparing a delicious pudding ablaze with brandy for dessert. Kitty singed her eyebrows while serving the flaming dishes, but she declared that the occasion deserved a little sacrifice.

Kosinsky and I were appointed a committee of two to go to Montreux and buy the fireworks, and Tex nominated himself to go along as guard. We bought several dozen rockets, some whirligigs, and a raft of packaged ladyfingers. With a little bribery we managed to get half a dozen "giant salutes," but we were warned not to fire them in town. We had a couple drinks then, and headed for the funic.

After the first stop we three had the car to ourselves. Tex was carrying the sackful of ladyfingers, while Tony and I shared the load of rockets and other stuff. I didn't think anything of it when Tex said he was going to sit in the back of the car, but if I hadn't been so drowsy I would have noticed he was up to something. As we passed the downcoming car at midpoint, I looked to see who was in it, and out of the tail of my eye saw Tex slip out to the rear platform.

He was back in a moment, and I was puzzled at the wide grin on his face until I heard the popping sputter of exploding ladyfingers diminishing down the hill. I thought at first that Tex had just pitched a lighted pack out on the wayside, but when we ground to an unscheduled halt I realized he had tossed the firecrackers into the other car as it went past. I expected the other conductor to come storming back to our car and confiscate all our fireworks, but nothing happened, and in a few moments we were under way again. Our conductor acted as though he had not heard the ruckus.

"Tex," I demanded when we were back at the hotel, "what did you do that for? You might have got somebody hurt."

"Aw heyull, Hickman, they was just little old ladyfingers," he replied. "Besides, I tossed them on the rear platform where they wouldn't hurt no one."

"I'll bet you we have a visit from the gendarmes this evening," I said. "The guy in the top station gave you an awful hard look when we went past him. Maybe the other conductor telephoned back when he got to the bottom."

"Nah!" Tex replied, "that suspicious bastard thinks that I'm the guy who stuck a wedge in the pulley last week. He looks at me like that all the time." He laughed. "Boy, was he burned up! First time in three years that the funic had been more'n two minutes off schedule."

I was right, though. Just before dark, while we were out on the terrace setting up our rockets, Kitty told me that a police officer was waiting in the lounge to see me.

"Here we go, boys!" I said. "Better round all the fellows up, Tony, if they want to see the fireworks. I'll stall the policeman and try to get him over to the other hotel. You watch us, Tex, and when you see us go you can signal Tony that the coast is clear. But wait—better watch from upstairs, Tex. If he sees you he might put the arm on you right now, since you're the prime suspect!''

I went in to face the law, confident that I could outmaneuver this provincial flatfoot, and Walt came along to see the fun. Tex ducked into the basement and went up the service stairs to his room, which looked out onto the street.

"We have a complaint that one of your people threw firecrackers in the funicular, Lieutenant," the police officer said. "It will be necessary for me to confiscate your fireworks as a consequence."

"You must realize, sir," I replied, "the seriousness of the thing you propose to do. You must understand that this is the sacred day of our country's independence. Custom requires that we discharge fireworks on this day, especially the sky rockets, which are the symbol of our triumph over the English. Even in our national anthem there are words about the rockets of liberty!"

"I understand, Lieutenant," the officer replied with a faint smile, "and I regret this very much. But I must carry out my instructions."

"Very well," I said stiffly, "but I will not take the responsibility. We will go to the other hotel and speak with Captain Hovecamp."

The policeman agreed to this suggestion readily enough, and we went out to his car and drove to Doug's hotel. I was a bit puzzled that the officials had taken an awfully long time to act upon this complaint. We had come up in the funic at about 2:30, and here was this cop arriving after eight in the evening. We rode the elevator up to Hovecamp's room without talking. In Doug's room the officer explained again what his orders were and why, and I was relieved to notice that he had his back to the window as he talked.

"I guess there's nothing we can do about it, Hickman. You'd better help this officer collect the stuff, and I'll see what I can do about getting your money back." He turned to the policeman and asked, "Would you have a glass of wine with us in honor of our Independence Day?"

"It is irregular to take a drink while one is on duty," the

policeman replied, "but since it is so special an occasion, I will be happy to drink with you."

I was afraid that the distant whistle and popping of rockets and the occasional boom of a salute would turn the police officer's attention to the window, but he was apparently too engrossed with wine and in Hovecamp's conversation to notice. Half an hour later, when the lawman and I returned to the Glion, I passed the word around to collect all fireworks. In a short while we had collected three packages of ladyfingers, two rockets without fuses, and a giant salute, also fuseless. Walt and Tony said that was absolutely all there was.

Seeming completely satisfied, the officer put the meager collection into a bag and thanked me for my cooperation. A dim light of comprehension was beginning to dawn in me. As he was about to leave, the policeman turned back and said, "I am very sorry there will be no fireworks tonight, Lieutenant. I spent one year studying in Washington, your capital city, and I enjoyed very much the displays near the Washington Monument on the Fourth of July."

"Perhaps another year, sir," I replied, grinning broadly and extending my hand. "May I escort you to your car?"

30

A dominating fact of our life in Switzerland was the urge nearly every one of us felt to plan an escape *back* into France, and ultimately to England. We certainly talked seriously, endlessly about it, and quite a number of actual attempts took place in the two months I was at Glion. It seems odd in retrospect, because there we were, home free, all of us having had a more or less hairy time of it getting there. But we all seemed to share a feeling of deep unease, sometimes amounting to guilt, at having it so easy while our buddies were still flailing away at a tough enemy.

Almost as notable as the escape syndrome itself was the difference in the approach to the escape problem between the American way and the English way. The Americans, Canadians, and Australians shared one view of the subject, while the British, New Zealanders, and South Africans held another, and quite different, one.

The Americans usually acted on impulse and took the simplest and most direct approach to escape. The British, on the other hand, favored rather elaborate routines involving careful planning and guile. I think that to the British the real point of the game was the style and form with which it was played, more than the result. All the escape attempts I knew of bore out the distinction to a remarkable degree: My own certainly did, but with a reverse twist.

165

It was during our quarantine at Bad Lostorf that I first began hearing the talk about escape from Switzerland. Somehow the preoccupation didn't surprise me, and I soon enough caught the fever myself. Shortly before I arrived in Glion, in late June, a typically American try took place. A bunch of about seven Americans and Canadians, out on the town of Montreux one night, finally became too rowdy for even the long-suffering Swiss. The police were called, but the boys saw them come in the front door of the bistro they were tearing up, so they ducked out the back. As the chase racketed up and down the streets of the sleeping town, an increasing number of citizens joined forces with the law. Our crowd suddenly decided that this was a good time to make for France and "freedom," so with a whoop they headed for the lakeshore, where hundreds of rowboats were pulled up for the night. With citizens and gendarmes in hot pursuit, the Allies piled into the handiest boat, scrounged a pair of oars, and shoved off as the posse thundered up the water's edge.

Those who were not rowing shouted jeers at the good folk on the shore, who for some reason made no effort to pursue them in other boats. One of the Canadians stood up in the bow of the boat, facing shoreward, and was shouting his views on what "you bloody Swiss can bloody well do with your—" when the boat came to an abrupt stop at the end of the long chain by which it was tethered to the quay. The Canadian and a couple of the others were toppled into the water by the jolt and had to swim back to shore. The rest sat sheepishly while the law pulled the boat in.

There were, of course, regular tries at what seemed the simplest route out, straight across the lake under cover of night. Such attempts were fairly frequent, but the swift current in the middle of the lake, coupled with strong night winds from the west, made the water too rough for such small boats as could be "borrowed" for the purpose. It was not uncommon to see two or three fellows straggle into the hotel in the wee hours of the morning, soaked through from the spray and bone tired from the unequal struggle with the lake. And sober. As far as I know, none of our crowd got out that way.

An enterprising New Zealander tried bluff to get around the guarded east end of the lake to the border. He rented a bicycle, and after studying the natives in their traditional Sunday garb, he outfitted himself accordingly. On the chosen day he tricked himself out in his lederhosen and rucksack and set off among the swarms of Sunday cyclists, reckoning himself as innocuously Swiss-looking as anyone else on the road. He had forgotten one important detail, however: His head had been shaved a few weeks earlier while he was in quarantine camp, and his telltale crop of new fuzz gave him away to the first policeman he passed. When he was escorted back to Glion, we were reminded again that both the police and the army were on the alert for any of our people who strayed from our defined area.

Actually we Americans, and I believe the others as well, were under orders to stay put in Switzerland. After the Normandy landings in June, our military made it a court-martial offense for any of us to return to France, judging reasonably enough that the French underground should be left unencumbered by restless fliers so they could concentrate on the main business of fighting Germans. Escape talking and planning went on undeterred, but actual attempts, with a few notable exceptions, were largely of the sort I've described, and unsuccessful. One of the notable exceptions was done in the best English style by a South African officer.

In early August a band of brigands came out of the French Alps and killed the small German garrison at the Swiss-French border village of Saint-Gingolph, which we could see directly across the lake from Montreux. The German reinforcements from Thonon retaliated ferociously the next day by killing every man they could catch in the French half of the village and by firing the buildings. Several of us were at the Pavillon the afternoon of the retaliation and saw the pall of smoke rising over the village.

The Saint-Gingolph ''massacre'' raised a cry in the Swiss press, and subscriptions were raised to buy flowers for the

dead and to take care of the survivors. We Allied troops
Glion raised money for our own floral tribute, to be sent
the memorial service scheduled to be held in the Swiss pa
of the village a few days later.

Neil, one of the South Africans who had earlier on e
corted me down the hiking trail, approached me the d
after the incident for assistance in a scheme he had work
out to turn the situation to advantage, an escape plan of t
British variety. He had arranged transportation for the A
lied bouquets, and having done that, he became the se
appointed representative of the Allies at the ceremon
Now, if I could assist him in getting suitable formal attire
morning coat if possible, and certainly a bowler hat,
would be pleased to arrange for me to go along to represe
the American crowd, and we would slip across to t
French side together. Since I didn't want to abandon r
own tentative plan, I declined Neil's offer, but helped h
scrounge up suitable garb.

Several days later I watched with the others as the car
van of flower-laden trucks drove out of Montreux. Towa
the rear of the column was our contribution, and standi
in the bed of the truck among the lilies, splendidly done
and looking appropriately solemn, was Neil. He got aw
with it, and I imagine he cut quite a figure ambling abc
France in that claw-hammer coat.

31

My own plan was shaping up against the anticipated lifting
of the escape ban. On August 15 the Allies landed in
southern France, and more and more Germans withdrew,
or were driven, from the part of France south of Lake
Geneva, until by the end of August the entire Haute-Savoie
was under the control of the Maquis and the Free French.

I must confess that by August my eagerness to get out of
Switzerland was prompted as much by a personal worry as
by the usual gung-ho patriotic reasons. Early on in Glion, I
learned that the managers of Swiss booze joints, from mom-
and-pop bistros on up to the posh watering places, allowed,
and even encouraged, Americans to sign for drinks. The
pay I received, even after deducting the allotment to my
wife, was ample but completely inadequate to sustain an
ebullient young American on the loose in Switzerland. God
only knows how many gallons of that marvelous Valais
wine I drank and dispensed freely right and left that glori-
ous summer, and I simply signed for much of it. *"Encore
du vin pour tous!"* was my battle cry.

By late July I began to worry seriously that I might be
kept on in the country until I had paid all my bills, which I
could only guess amounted to two or three months' pay. The
prospect of being kept behind in Switzerland after all the

others had been repatriated was too bleak to contemplat
so I began to scheme seriously.

A few days after the August landings in Southern Franc
we Americans got unofficial permission from our embas
in Bern to take off at our own risk. My plan was simply
go off for a week's visit at the home of Denise's mothe
She lived in a chalet near the border town of Morgin
south of the lake, and I figured that one sunny day Deni
and I would go out for a walk and I would simply nip
across the border. With my police pass in order, and wi
permission to be out of Montreux for a week, I was to go
Morgins on the twenty-third, where I was to be met l
Denise and her mother. From there on it would be a simp
matter.

But my English friend Gordon Fraser urged his own pla
upon me. After considerable cautious investigation, a p
vate group in the neighboring town of Vevey, engaged
smuggling out Frenchmen, had accepted Gordon as a pa
senger on their underground railroad, and he was certain l
could get me accepted as well. I agreed to give it a try, a
after a secret interview I was likewise accepted. So I aba
doned my simple American plan for this much more i
triguing British one. I liked and admired this Englishm
and relished the prospect of his company on this caper.

Money was a problem, since I always spent mine as fa
as I got it and Gordon simply did not get much. So I got
idea and made a deal with Gordon. I would go to Bern, g
an advance on next month's pay on the strength of n
approved holiday visit, and split the money with Gordo
He would then draw from RAF stores a pair of high-t
shoes for me to replace my light civilian shoes.

On August 24 Gordon made the final arrangements l
pulling out, and I went to Bern. The disbursing offic
looked at me suspiciously and asked if I was planning
skip the country. I replied, "Now, why in the world wou
I want to pull a fool stunt like that?" Apparently he cou
think of no good reason, because he handed me the fou
dollars I had requested.

That evening I made final preparations. I wrote a lett

to the American military attaché explaining that I was leaving to rejoin my combat unit, and declaring I had no intention of welching on the several bills I had outstanding, but would pay them "in due course." It was my primary military duty, I explained, to rejoin my unit at the earliest possible opportunity (never mind that I didn't have the foggiest idea where the hell my unit was at the time).

I packed into my rucksack what extra clothes I had, along with a dozen packs of cigarettes. My hardest job was persuading the other fellows in the hotel that no, indeed, I had no intention of skipping out. I hoped to discourage them for a few days, anyway, because I was afraid that a mass exodus at that time might arouse the Swiss police, alert the border people, and mess up the escape Gordon and I had planned.

So we had everything arranged. The American girl, Elaine, exchanged our few good Swiss francs for a bale of lovely, worthless French francs, and all we had to do was make our rendezvous undetected the next morning. We took elaborate precautions to sneak our knapsacks out of our respective hotels late that night and then spent the remainder of the night in a room we had taken in Vevey under assumed names. Early the next morning we headed for the meeting place, an out-of-the-way cafe down by the lakefront in Vevey.

We stayed in a back room of the cafe in company with an increasing number of uncommunicative young men who, we concluded, were to be our fellow travelers. We did learn that they were French, and that as refugees they had spent the past two or more years at hard labor as wards of the Swiss government. They had finally escaped and were now on the last leg of their return to France and the Resistance.

For about two hours nothing happened, we just sat there. I finally decided to go up the street and buy some matches, since we had forgotten to bring a supply along and none could be had in the cafe. Gordon thought he had better not go out on the street, since he was wearing his RAF battle jacket and might be spotted by the police. I was wearing flannel slacks and a light sport shirt, so I would not likely be noticed.

Just as I got up to the main street and was about to cross over to the tobacco kiosk, I saw an unbelievable sight—six or seven Americans from my hotel and two Canadian fellows with them, all tricked out in traveling clothes and rucksacks, moving purposefully down the street in a body, toward me. Two things marked them blatantly as Allied escapees: To a man the thin crop of hair on their heads proclaimed that they had fairly recently had their heads shaved; and the garb of their leader, a short Pole from Detroit, screamed "foreigner!" He had on a Tyrolean hat and was smoking his enormous, ornamented Swiss (tourist) pipe.

I was so amazed to see this troupe at high noon on the main street of Vevey, way out of bounds already and clearly bent on getting farther out, that I didn't duck soon enough. The Pole spotted me and hailed me loudly in English, so as quickly as I could I got the whole group herded into the relative security of a coffee shop. These fellows had suspected that I was going to bug out, and when one of them saw me slip out the night before with my pack, they took that as a signal to shove off too. So they had assembled at a bistro, made plans while they got loaded with wine, went back to the hotel and packed, then tramped down to Montreux.

Around midnight they expropriated an unchained rowboat and started to row across the lake to the French side. Out toward the middle they hit the rough water and headed back for shore rather than risk swamping the overloaded boat. By this time it was morning, and they had been swept so far along that when they touched land again it was in Vevey rather than Montreux. They abandoned the boat and for the past half-hour had been wandering around Vevey trying to decide what to do. They declared they wanted to go along with me, but I nixed that one. Instead, I gave them the name and address of the person who had arranged our escape, told them for God's sake to quit parading around the streets, and left them. I decided after that encounter to stay in hiding. That bunch would certainly succeed in stirring up the police.

At about six o'clock that afternoon things began to liven up. A fellow came in and gave us our instructions: We were to follow him, spaced out single file at intervals of twenty yards, and we were to look casual. Out the back door we filed, down an alley, into the front door of a department store, out the back door. On and on went this singularly conspicuous convoy of evenly spaced, synchronously paced, haversacked men.

After a half-hour of this curious snake dance through Vevey's stores and streets, we wound up bunched together in an alley beside a large flatbed truck piled high with empty crates. These crates had been so loaded as to create a sizable hollow space in the middle, into which the lot of us were crammed. Then the opening at the rear was plugged with more crates, the whole issue was lashed down, and off we went. Gordon and I assumed that we would be driven directly across the border, and that shortly we would have the free road ahead of us.

But we had underestimated the caution of our liberators. After an hour or so of jostling travel, the rear crates were removed and we crawled out. It was early evening, and the towering thunderheads gave promise of a stormy night. We were at the foot, on the south side, of a mountain range whose ridge ran east and west, to the south of the lake. The word finally got through to Gordon and me that we were still in Switzerland, and were to go the rest of the way afoot.

The leader of the Frenchmen chattered briefly at his fellows, then headed straight up the side of the mountain, the others strung out behind him. Since we had no notion where we were, Gordon and I figured we had better trail along. So up the hill we went, and the hellish night began.

I was winded before we had gone two hundred yards, because the hill was steep and the pace was geared to the ruggedness of those Frenchmen. By the end of the first hour I was done in completely. We were just well started up that damned mountain when the rain hit us, driving, icy buckets of it. A short eternity later it was pitch-dark, so between the cold rain, the slippery footing, and my night blindness, that trek to freedom became a nightmare. A flash of lightning would occasionally show the world with a dead light, and I would see the Frenchmen strung out ahead, frozen for an instant in attitudes of exertion.

I had the odd feeling that I was the only one working and struggling, because in those brief flashes I saw only soundless, motionless postures, each time different but each time only suggesting motion I could not see. One time I was looking back when the lightning flashed and I saw Gordon, arms and shoulders stretched forward, eyes bulging and mouth gaping. In that instant I saw his foot slip and he went down on one knee, his hands clawing at the dirt ahead of him, pulling himself on. I have never seen a man in so desperate a posture of strain; he must have been going through hell. Yet through all that fantastic night I never heard a word of complaint from him. In the brief snatches of conversation we had, he would not even admit that the going was rough.

We managed to hang on to that frantic group of Frenchmen through those several hours of darkness, rain, and mountain, but I don't know how. Nor, under the circumstances, do I know precisely why. There was only the drenched darkness shattered by occasional blinding flashes of lightning, dead fatigue, and the stupidly fixed idea that I must at all costs keep going. After a time (I judged it to be close to midnight), we came to a halt. The rain had stopped, but the sky was overcast and it was still black dark, with only rare and more distant, flashes of lighting. We halted for a seemingly endless time while two of the Frenchmen went ahead to reconnoiter. It became very still, and several times I thought surely everyone had left me and I had not heard them go. Once I called out softly, and Gordon replied no five feet from me.

It was during that halt that I think I experienced my absolute depth of physical discomfort. I was dressed to suit a loafer in summery Montreux, with my cotton sport shirt and light slacks. After the heroic exertions of the earlier evening, my body was now undergoing the shock of adjusting to sudden cold immobility. The upper part of my body was wretchedly, hopelessly chilled, and I shivered so violently at times that I almost lost my balance. A cold wind, soaking wet clothes, and a body hot from exertion should have added up to pneumonia, but I didn't even catch a cold.

After a time the scouts came back, and some decision was reached in a confab among the Frenchmen. By the time we started off again, this time to the left and slightly downhill, the clouds had broken and I was able to see dimly in the starlight. We went only about a quarter of a mile to a small stone building with a high-peaked roof nestled on the side of the mountain. We went straight to the building and walked into what my nose told me was a cow barn. We were, I understood, to stay there until morning and make the rest of our trip by daylight. I was not sorry. The barn at least got us out of that miserable, cold wind, and the six or eight cows tied in their stalls did provide a bit of warmth. Most of all I was glad for the rest, and to have done with the infuriating business of flailing about in the dark.

One of the Frenchmen produced a candle and lit it, by God only knows what means, and we set about bedding down. That was no simple task, because the place had not been cleaned out for at least a year, and the cows were knee-deep in their own mire. There was a bare minimum of space between the business ends of the beasts and the wall, and so it was something of a trick to scrounge up enough dry straw and fodder to make a place suitable for reclining.

We had barely gotten settled when I heard a splashing of water from one of the cows down the line followed by a torrent of outraged French, the sound of a boot connecting with the side of a cow, and the animal's surprised "Oooof!" Having been raised on a farm, and therefore wise to the habits of cattle, I had taken the necessary precautions about situating myself, so I was undisturbed in my sleep.

There was only the barest suggestion of light in the world when I was awakened by the movement and voices of the

Frenchmen. Gordon was already up, and we were both fairly fit, considering the ordeal of the evening before, and the fact that our clothes were still wet. One of the others had a tin cup and was rousing a cow with the intention of milking her. The way he went about it showed he was a novice, so I undertook to do the honors. Several of the fellows gathered around as I soothed a likely looking animal and started to clean off her udder.

But I got no further than that, because just then a door opposite the one we had entered, opened and an old fellow in rustic clothes came among us. He apparently was the farmer who owned these animals, and he invited us all over to his house for breakfast. The trip was very simple, because all we had to do was step through the door and there we were. The other half of that small stone building, the smaller half, was kitchen and living room for this farmer. He and his wife slept in the loft over the cow shed. It was all very cozy, but also very pungent. He had a nice fire going, and he offered us each a cup of milk. But the smell of the barn was so strong that the milk tasted of it, so one sip was all I could manage.

Our leader parleyed with the farmer a bit, and then we all tramped off into a sparkling clear dawn. The morning half of this journey was as pleasant as the evening half had been hideous. The ground was slippery underfoot, but as day broke with a promise of summer warmth, nothing could seriously disturb my spirits. We slithered along for upward of two hours before our leader called a halt. There was some question whether we had crossed the border.

We had been descending our mountain, and now, half a mile ahead and only a little below us, we could see a sort of roadblock across a road that wound up the valley to the west. The question was, Swiss or French? And if French, was it manned by Germans or by the French Resistance?

Two of the Frenchmen went on ahead to scout, and after a bit we could hear one of our men in a call-conversation with the one fellow we could see at the roadblock. A brief bit of shouting evidently assured our men that the guard at the gate was on our side, because they hollered at us in

urn, and the rest of the Frenchmen started off at a run for
he gate. At the roadblock there was a great deal of excited
hatter, dancing about, and kissing of cheeks. Gordon and
  were welcomed to France with a traditional hug and a
vhiskery kiss on the cheek by each one of our French
ompanions. After twelve hours of waiting in Vevey and
welve miserable hours on the side of that damned mountain,
ve were in France.

I was proud of Gordon and myself for our achievement:
Not only had we got to France, we had kept pace with the
vell-conditioned Frenchmen in the bargain. I considered
hat quite an accomplishment, and thought how very clever
Gordon and I had been to pull it off.

Three days later we ran across two Americans, from the
ther hotel in Glion, who had come out of Switzerland the
"American" way. Having decided one evening to decamp,
hey had a bottle of wine and went to bed. The next
norning they had a leisurely breakfast, then packed their
elongings. By eleven o'clock they were ready to go, so
hey called the mad Glion cabbie and had him drive them to
Morgins. He pointed the way to them and they simply
valked the few remaining yards into France. Their trip
rom Glion to France took them just one comfortable hour!

PART THREE

Heading
Back
to
the
War

32

France, and freedom again! The road, winding between towering Alps, beckoned us westward toward England, and I fondly believed that in two or three days we would be there. As we ambled along that warm, bright morning I pictured myself regaling the fellows—Johnny Hoefker, Frank Dillon, Dick Booze, Jack Chapin, and the others—with my mad tale. It never occurred to me that the squadron might not be in England anymore, or that the replacement rate during the past few killing months might have completely changed the character of the outfit. But I could no more imagine any of my friends being killed than I could imagine myself being dead.

We hitched a ride to where the road ran close along the lakeshore, and we then loafed on westward, enjoying our freedom. The weather was flawless August, the lake danced in the sunlight, the birds sang, and we were free. It made not a damn bit of difference to anyone whether by day's end we had traveled west, south, or east, or whether we made no progress at all in any direction. Day's end, week's end, the end of the month—no one cared, the natives were hospitable, and the swans glided serenely along just off shore.

That was *real* freedom. As far as our two air forces and families were concerned, Gordon and I were out of action and presumed safely interned in Switzerland. Our people in Switzerland presumed we were in France, but we were out of *their* hair.

There was only one flaw in that otherwise perfect condition: We had a direction we *felt* we had to go. We both had this thing—"sense of duty" describes it as well as anything—that compelled us on to find our people and rejoin the rat race. But we didn't have to be in a big hurry about it.

Gordon and I discovered during that first day that most of the rumors we had heard in Switzerland as to the whereabouts of the U.S. Army in France were false, as were the "instructions" the local French types gave us. We walked and rode to Evian up on the lake, and from there westward to Thonon: no U.S. Army. Later that same day we managed to get a ride as far as Annecy, where the Americans were supposed to have a headquarters: no army. By the time we got to Annecy it was late, so we got a hotel room, were served, to our astonishment, a complete five-course dinner, and turned in. And it was all free—we were the "liberators"!

The following day began quietly enough. We were up around eight in the morning and had a leisurely breakfast, intending to do some sight-seeing in that famous resort area before moving on in our search for the elusive army. We had not walked far, however, before a fellow approached us and asked if we would accompany him to Maquis headquarters. We were eager to have a look at these famously resourceful French fighting people, so we went with him.

At "headquarters" we were taken in tow by a group of young women, the Maquis equivalent of our WACs, and given a briefing on Maquis operations, which I listened to, I must admit, with only half an ear. The girls were all attractive, and one, a Parisian, was quite beautiful. The bright-eyed beauty told us the Maquis were in effective control of the Department of Haute-Savoie and had set up a network of roadblocks and strongholds throughout the region. They were prepared to turn over control to and cooperate with the advanced Allied forces—and, inquired our briefing officer, did we know when they would arrive, Lieutenant? I looked into those big hazel eyes and hoped that the liberators would manage to stay away at least a few days more. I felt encouraged in my belief that she had the same hope.

One point the lady made with very strong feeling was the refusal of the Germans to treat the Maquis as a bona fide army under the rules of war. What this meant, she explained, was that captured Maquis regulars, even when identified as such, were often tortured by the Gestapo to get information from them, or brutally disfigured as a deterrent to other Maquis.

She showed us files containing photographs of the broken, scarred bodies of both men and women who had been tortured. One particularly gruesome picture showed the face of a very young-looking girl with an U-shaped cut on the scalp that laid the top front of her skull bare. With each photograph were pages of written material documenting the case. According to our Parisian Maquis, the Gestapo stopped short of no barbarity either to obtain evidence or to discourage collaboration with the underground.

We learned another interesting thing that morning. On the Maquis's Most-Despised list, second only to the Germans, was the FFI, or French Forces of the Interior, the touted Resistance outfit whose insignia was the Cross of Lorraine. The FFI—unlike the Maquis—was recognized by the French government-in-exile. It appeared to me that not only were the French incapable of fighting as a nation, but they were unable to reconcile their differences even under the desperate circumstances of underground resistance.

Except for the grim briefings, we spent a very pleasant morning. We had arrived in Annecy while our Maquis hosts were tasting their first major victory since their long, hard fight had begun. And now, with the Americans driving up from the south, complete liberation was in sight. In high spirits, they vented their enthusiasm on Gordon and me. It is a measure of their exuberance that they were willing to see embodied in us, as sorry-looking a pair of walking pilots as ever dumped a chute, the mighty forces of Great Britain and the United States, joined in an enterprise of liberation. By noon quite a sizable group was assembled in the headquarters mess to do us honor. The complete absence of gold braid and brass made it possible for Gordon and me to relax and enjoy the camaraderie that pervaded the gathering.

We were hardly into the noon meal, however, and I was just at the point where I had established a very adequate working vocabulary with the charming Parisian, when we were all attracted by shouting in the square outside. The building we were in faced upon a park about the size of a city block, bordered by streets; and the dining room, on the second floor, had a balconied window looking out on the square. I followed the others to the window to see what the uproar was all about—and there it was, the U.S. Army, Stars and Stripes in the lead.

The detachment consisted of four jeeps, each with a trailer, and an oversized American flag rippled from a short pole fastened to the hood of the lead jeep. A couple of soldiers occupied each jeep, and as they rounded the far end of the square, coming back toward us after going around the square, I made a break for the stairs. I got into the square just as the lead jeep turned into the street in front of the headquarters building. It was apparent that in spite of the growing crowd swarming around the slow-moving vehicles, the Americans did not intend to stop. The lieutenant in the lead jeep kept waving to the people, but shaking his head and signaling his driver to keep moving.

I pushed through the crowd, calling to them to stop. The lieutenant heard my Americanese, and when he spotted me he waved back and told the driver to stop. We shook hands and I explained who I was and what I was doing here. He said that they were a reconnaissance patrol from the 45th Division, headquartered at Grenoble, with orders to go to the Swiss border and back to Grenoble before midnight, at which time the division was moving out. But he did not want to offend these enthusiastic allies.

After a three-cornered parley, with Gordon and me as

interpreters, we worked out a compromise. The patrol would continue on its mission but would stop for an official welcome on the way back, later in the afternoon. Gordon and I were to remain as a sort of hostage against the patrol's return. So in a din of shouting, the dazed GIs and their lieutenant went on their way, and Gordon and I, too excited to finish lunch, rounded up the beauteous Maquis, located a pleasant sidewalk cafe, and proceeded to celebrate. I'm afraid our poorly concealed joy at this turn of events was not very flattering to our companions, and I tried to explain why we thought it necessary to take the opportunity to move on.

The hullabaloo started up again as soon as the jeeps were back. I had gotten the word that a big shot in the Maquis would be honored to welcome the American forces in person at his place a few miles out of town, and I so informed the lieutenant. This person, it was explained emphatically, could not be denied without risk of a serious breach between the liberators and the Resistance, so out to his place we went, and there drank toasts of straight brandy from water tumblers. A GI standing near me stared at his glass and muttered, "Jesus! Nothing to drink for six weeks and all of a sudden I'm drinking brandy like water!"

Back in town a rare welcome had been prepared, a banquet with forty or fifty people seated and a couple hundred standing and watching. Gordon and I shared honored places with the soldiers, the mayor, and some other notables. They all had two heads, and about all I can remember about the banquet is that we were served the largest steaks I had ever seen, and at each place was a bottle of brandy. At some stage in the proceedings we got back to the jeeps, each man clutching his bottle, and amid a lot of noisy leave-taking, we roared off into a drizzly night.

33

The ride to Grenoble might have been two hours or it might have been six. I was jammed into the rear seat of the second jeep with two GIs and slept most of the way. At one point during the trip the soldiers told me that on their way to the Swiss border they had picked up a bunch of other American airmen, three of whom had been in Switzerland. One of the three was Joe Coss, the sergeant who had saved me from getting the Purple Heart in Switzerland. The other two Swiss internees were the ones who had simply hailed the taxi out. They got as far as Thonon, and instead of going on looking for the army, they had waited and let the army find them. The rest of the Americans had been hiding out with the French, some for nearly a year.

The roads were wet from the drizzle, the lieutenant was in a hurry to get back to Grenoble, and the jeeps as well as the trailers were overloaded with the soldiers and the added Air Corps flotsam they had accumulated during the day. And there was not a sober man in the crowd, unless it was the lieutenant. We had been warned that at certain points along the way there would be roadblocks at which we must stop. Whether we stopped at any of them I couldn't say, but I do know that twice we barreled past armed men at what seemed to be control points, with a chorus of shouts of "*Américain!*" from the passengers. At one of them I heard two shots, quickly lost in the shouts of laughter and general hubbub.

We brawled into Grenoble late that night, just as the division was moving out, so we refugees took over quarters vacated by the departing troops and slept it off. Next morning we were put aboard a train headed south, and although I'd been under the impression it was going all the way to the south coast, it stopped about a third of the way down. It seems the bridge had been blown up in the recent hostilities, so that was the end of the line. We were then loaded into a six-by-six and taken to a very orderly army bivouac, where we were fed supper and put up for the night.

In the morning, early, we had breakfast and were thoroughly interrogated by a major, one at a time. He did not let on what he was trying to learn from us, probably because he didn't know, but he went about his business briskly enough, and when he was finished he gave each of us a slip of paper saying we had been interrogated. We were to travel the rest of the way in a supply truck that was deadheading back to the beachhead.

Just about noon, after an early lunch, we took off on that mad, slamming ride to the Riviera, and after dark we got there. We bowled through villages, charged across flat country, and careened around mountains where the narrowness of the road and the sheer drops had my hair standing on end. By the time we got to the beachhead I was completely unnerved.

Whatever it was I expected to find at a beachhead, it was certainly not the sight that greeted me at Saint-Tropez. The whole area was lighted up by powerful floodlights—not just patches and parts, but the whole damned two-mile square of it. All around were huge piles of supplies, mountains of boxes, crates, and drums of all descriptions, with men and trucks and tractors scurrying about like agitated ants. We finally got directions to a place where we could sleep, and the next morning we found that we had located, luckily, next to a mess tent. After breakfast we drifted back to a wreck of buildings, set above and a short distance back from the beach, which served as headquarters for the whole insane beachhead operation. There we got word that we would be taken back to Naples in one of the big landing craft that carried supplies in to the beach. A short Mediterranean cruise sounded OK to me, so I propped myself against a building to soak in some of that fabled Riviera sunshine and to await developments.

After a while I struck up a conversation with one of the GIs around the place and was told that those boats they had in mind for us took *eleven days* to make the run to Naples, and that they were very uncomfortable, pitching like fury even in a moderate sea. This information snapped me awake, and from some recess in my being there sprang, full-grown and vital, a determination to fly to Naples.

I realized that it would take some doing to get a flight organized, so I went into action. A count revealed that there were now nineteen of us refugees from orderly warfare: three assorted British Colonial Indian infantrymen, turned up from somewhere; an English navy flier who had been shot down only a few days before; a couple of British aircrewmen; Gordon Fraser; and twelve of us American officers and enlisted men, all Air Corps.

I looked for someone to answer my questions and listen to my proposition, and found him in the person of a kindly, white-haired colonel. As near as I could make out, he was in sole command of the score of mimeograph machines that were clacking away in one of the headquarters rooms keeping pace with the general pandemonium. Where could I find Air Corps field headquarters? I asked. They had pulled out early that morning for a location just north of Marseilles, the colonel told me, to a field called Salon. He would try to find out precisely where it was, but a half-hour of phoning and asking around netted him zero. He seemed embarrassed at thus having to admit that to all appearances we had lost an entire air force, so I pressed my advantage. Could he give me a truck with a driver and a map of the south of France so we could set out to find the Air Corps? He said he could, and admitted with an effort at jollity that *he* would like to know where they were too.

Then, being a man concerned in a professional way with such things, he remembered that military personnel must have orders signed by a competent authority before they could use military air transportation. Would he prepare such orders for me? He was sorry that he could not, inasmuch as such orders had to be signed by an Air Corps officer, and he was Artillery, or Signal Corps, or some such unlikely thing. Well, then, I persisted, would he prepare orders, leave them unsigned, and let me have copies, together with the mimeograph stencil, so that when I caught up with a "proper authority" I would require only a signature?

This was a happy solution, and it galvanized the old colonel into action. He could, by this device, help us, get rid of us, employ his trade to the general benefit, and, by giving me the stencil, completely absolve himself of complicity in this irregular business. But only the fliers could go on the orders. The ground force soldiers would have to go by surface transportation.

I quickly collected the full names of my motley company, and immediately the good colonel had typewriter and mimeograph machines in motion. In a matter of minutes I had a manila envelope containing the stencil and twenty copies of those worthless orders listing my rag-tail international air force whose sole mission was to find the U.S. Air Corps in southern France. Soon I had a map of sorts and a truck with a driver. This trip promised to be somewhat more comfortable for me than the run down from Grenoble, since I, as self-appointed officer-in-charge and navigator, sat in front with the driver. With the colonel's relieved good wishes, we set out briskly to find the only airport that was shown on my vintage map in the vicinity of Marseilles.

Our route from Saint-Tropez to Marseilles gave us frequent glimpses of the sea, and since it was another gorgeous day, the trip was mostly pleasant—except for the first large town we hit.

Toulon was a startling sight. I had forgotten until we were in the town that the Germans had elected to make a last-ditch stand there and had surrendered only a few days before. The marks of violence were upon the town, but more terrible were the shocked stillness of the place and the pervasive stink of death in the hot summer air. A few miles beyond the town we overtook a four-mile-long column of weary German soldiers being shepherded along by French troops in American uniforms. The crack of rifle fire and the thumping drum of submachine guns kept the column moving at a pace more suited to the Frenchmen than to the beaten Germans. It was not a pretty thing to witness.

By midafternoon we were prowling country roads and lanes in search of that elusive airfield, which we knew was somewhere nearby. In a clearing just off a byroad we found a U.S. Signal Corps unit complete with communications trailer, mess tent, and second lieutenant. After I'd made my howdys and explained our presence, I asked the young officer if he knew where Air Corps had located. Sorry, he didn't know. Could he tell me where Salon airfield was? Gee, no, he didn't know. Well, how about pinpointing our present location on our map so we could be sure we were on the right track? Stammering and blushing, the lieutenant took me aside and admitted that he and his unit had been wandering around lost for the past three days. They not only didn't know where the Air Corps was, they had lost the whole damned U.S. Army.

At last our truck trundled up the right lane and we saw an airfield wide and flat before us. But what we saw on close inspection was discouraging: Small groups of engineer troops were working over the ground around the hangar area with mine detectors, and no sign of an airplane of any sort was to be seen.

As we debated what our next move should be, a C-47 appeared above the field, circled once, and landed. We raced out onto the field on the trail of the landing plane and pulled our truck up beside it as it taxied to a stop on the far side of the field. This was a weary-looking old crate, with extra-large doors on the side. The crew of the plane opened the doors, worried a ramp into place, and with a great deal of sweat and swearing worked a spanking new jeep out of the plane and down the ramp to the ground. The jeep was equipped with a driver.

My riffraff command and I watched this operation in puzzled silence. A still more wonderful sight followed the jeep down the ramp: a major, showing Judge Advocate General insignia, and wearing a class A uniform, complete with grommeted hat, swagger stick and penciled moustache. He was no taller than I, and about my build, but the manner he affected made him Mr. Big.

The pilot of the plane, a lieutenant colonel, and his copilot had climbed down from the cockpit and were looking at something under the wing, paying no attention to any of us.

I started forward to address the pilot to ask him if he would fly us out. I was halfway over to him when the major brought me up short with his demand, "Who are these men?" Although I wasn't looking at him when he spoke, I knew he was addressing me, so feeling like a schoolboy caught in a silly mistake, I went over to him and explained who I was, what we were doing there, and where we wanted to go.

If he was impressed by my story, he didn't show it. He demanded to see my identification, so I showed him the ID card that had been issued to me in Switzerland. The major looked the card over, handed it back, and asked if I was the ranking officer among this rabble scum. He didn't actually say "rabble scum," but his tone left no doubt how he viewed us ragamuffin heroes. I said that I was the ranking officer, knowing he would have the devil's own time proving I was not.

"All right, Lieutenant, line your men up," he snapped.

Why, I thought in amazement, this pompous ass is going to examine each one of these men and maybe the plane will leave without us!

"Sir," I explained, "most of these men have been hiding out with the French the better part of the year, and so they don't have any official identification. We are proceeding to Naples for interrogation."

Without hesitating the major went on, "Will you vouch for these men personally, Lieutenant?" I said I would. The major started to turn away when his steel-trap mind came up with a clincher.

"You may not realize it, Lieutenant, but you are required to have orders to fly in military aircraft. Where do you propose to get orders in this place?"

So at last I got revenge of a sort on this insufferable little martinet. I brandished my manila envelope, opened the flap, and pulled out the top copy of our phony orders just far enough so the major could see the letterhead and the list of names, but not far enough so he could see the blank space where a signature belonged.

"And I have a copy of these orders for each of my men," I offered as I stuffed the paper back into the envelope. The bluff worked. The major turned to the pilot and ordered "Colonel, fly these men to Rome!" With this he climbed into the jeep, motioned to his driver, and without a backward glance they went off in the general direction of Paris.

With the major out of the way, I went over to the pilot and asked him civilly if he could see his way to giving us a lift in the direction of Naples. The pilot, younger than the major, was rangy and easygoing. He said he thought they might manage a lift as far as Rome, and then he asked casually if I would mind showing him a copy of my orders. This time I pulled the paper all the way out of the envelope and handed it to him. He glanced at the mimeographed sheet, looked at me, and grinned.

"Okay," he said, "let's go."

34

We stayed that night with the colonel's squadron at their field a few miles out of Rome, and the next day he scheduled a flight to take us on to Naples. He and his men had been uninterested in me and my motley crew until I told him over drinks that night that I was from near Fort Wayne, Indiana. Interest picked up at once. This squadron, like many other Troop Carrier outfits in the European theater, had staged at Baer Field, near Fort Wayne. Fine town, great people! Best soldier's town in the U.S. Yes, sir, nothing too good for a boy from Fort Wayne! When I explained that we were anxious to get on to Naples, where theater headquarters was, the CO was happy to oblige.

The Rome-Naples flight was a short one, and we were set down without much ceremony in a large airfield that handled mainly transport planes. C-47s, C-46s, and occasional heavy bombers were landing and taking off continually, and there were clusters of the olive drab transports parked all around the field. It was here that our crowd had a parting of the ways. The British fellows decided to look up their own people and seek their destinations by RAF facilities. So Gordon and I shook hands and agreed on a vague plan to meet in London. It didn't work out, and I haven't seen him since. The rest of us were directed to theater headquarters at Caserta, about twenty miles north-east of Naples.

This headquarters occupied a monumental palace built, I was told, around the end of the eighteenth century. As a palace it must once have been fabulous, but as the nucleus of a military effort, long after the heyday of the Bourbon royalty that had built the place, it looked drab and tired. This headquarters area was all the confusion and disarray I had ever seen in connection with the military service at war, compounded a hundred times over. The general atmosphere suited, or maybe derived from, the palace-heap that was the hub of the careening universe called the Mediterranean Theater of Operations. The place swarmed with brass and WACs, the former elderly and ineffectual-looking, the latter young and good-looking.

We spent a tiring and frustrating two days enduring yet another interrogation, arranging for pay, and getting at least a partial issue of uniform clothing. No one seemed to know where anything was, nor how we could get there when we found out, and when we did get there the people were uninterested in helping us. Dirty, carrion combat types we were, intruding on *their war!*

By the time we had slogged our way through the official routine, it became clear that most of the other men were not as eager as I to push on. This seemed to them a good spot to loaf for a while, and several of the pilots were determined to wangle a "rest cure" at the fabled Island of Capri, which was being used exclusively as a rest center for fliers. Only one of the crowd, my old Switzerland buddy Joe Coss, was as anxious as I to get back to England. From Naples onward we were constant traveling companions, and I came to appreciate him even more as a real eager beaver.

Once finished at Caserta, Joe and I took our leave of the rest and bummed a ride into Naples to arrange our transportation to England with the Air Transport Command booking office. It sounds like peacetime travel, and worked about the same way. They ran a booking system much like a commercial airline's, even to the point of having a regular ticket office in town.

The prospects of an early flight with ATC were discouraging, because with the priority they gave us we could be bumped by the lowliest GI bent on any kind of foolishness he had orders to perpetrate. Nevertheless, regardless of how long he might have to wait, a prospective passenger had to be constantly on hand at short notice once he had booked. If a person missed his assigned flight, for whatever reason, he was listed as a no-show and his chances of ever getting a ride were slim indeed.

We were told that it would be at least eight days, possibly ten, before we could expect to get out by ATC. We disliked the idea of such a long wait, but had our names listed for scheduling anyway. We looked around Naples a bit, but the town was so drab and depressing we headed back for our billets. On the way Joe suggested we go to the airfield and see if we could scrounge a ride out on one of the assortment of troop carrier and hospital planes based there. The idea appealed to me, so we collected our gear and went out to the base.

The sergeant in base operations told us we could expect no official help on our undertaking, so we started the round of the field. Each cluster of planes was a different unit, and each had a sort of field operations section. We must have talked with twenty operations officers on our circuit of that enormous field, and we got not the slightest encouragement from any of them. About four o'clock we were in a canteen having a Coke. I was tired, fed up, and discouraged, and so sick of the place I was willing to go away in any direction. I would have left an hour before to try some other angle, but Joe persuaded me to hang on. Something might turn up, he argued.

And it did. Joe found someone there in the canteen whom he knew from years back, and in a few minutes he came back excited, yelling, "We've got a ride!" and hustled me out of the canteen. His friend had a friend whose plane was just getting ready to take off for a field somewhere west of Tunis in North Africa, and he thought he might get us aboard. The three of us ran to this dispersal close by the canteen and found the C-47 warming up.

After a flurry of conversation with a fellow in the doorway of the plane, while we stood on the ground in the dusty prop-wash, and a brief consultation between this guy and the pilot, the man in the doorway shouted, "Okay, goddamit, get aboard!" We clambered in, and although we got a surly reception and were studiously ignored the whole flight, at least we were on our way and out of that miserable place. The thought crossed my mind once that now we were no-shows; but, thought I further, New places, new schedules!

35

As we winged south daylight faded, and it was night by the time we landed. From what I could see, both from the air and on the ground, this field was in a flat desert, a way station to nowhere. It was cold, and when we went into the operations shack we learned the worst. This was indeed a way station, a sort of servicing, fueling, and freight transfer terminal. It served both the Royal Air Force and the U.S. Air Corps, and as a consequence was manned jointly by British and American personnel. The bad part was that there was no passenger scheduling from here; it was strictly an ATC freight-handling operation.

I had already learned that the ATC, run for the most part by commercial airlines people in uniform, operated in a very businesslike manner. In contrast with the casualness of the Troop Carrier outfits we had encountered, the ATC did everything by the book, from the handling of passenger schedules and weight-loading of freight to the elaborate preflight checking of engines.

The sergeant at operations with whom I talked advised me to catch a ride back to Naples if I could, and get back on the ATC schedule. He said that even if he did try to get us booked out on the ATC passenger flight coming through, we would be spotted as no-shows and turned down. This was all very discouraging, especially since the plane that had brought us in had long since refueled and gone on its way. We went to the snack bar for coffee and an emergency conference and there discovered two comrades from Switzerland who had somehow gotten this far and were likewise stuck. They had been there the whole day. Nobody had any fresh ideas, so after a bit I headed back to operations for another try. It seemed inconceivable to me that we could not be worked in, given all the planes passing through the place. The no-nonsense orderliness of the place, however, was a reminder of the ATC way of doing things.

Then I had another of my lucky breaks. In the operations room I noticed an RAF officer marking numbers on the control board and had the feeling I knew him. I asked one of the British airmen what the officer's name was, but the name he told me didn't register. Finally it hit me, when I had a look at the Englishman's profile. He had been adjutant of the RAF 165 Squadron that I had served with on detached service for a couple of months the previous fall. His name hadn't registered simply because I had never heard it mentioned. He, like all RAF squadron adjutants, was called simply "Adge," just as the intelligence officer was always addressed as "Spy." This particular adge and I had never been close companions, but he had been on several pub crawls with the gang of us fliers in the jeep I had at my disposal.

Sure enough, this was the 165 Squadron adge. He recognized me, there in that desert outpost, as soon as the airman called his attention to me. He came over, called me by name, and shook hands cordially. We talked awhile, and I told him where I had been and what had happened. And when I told him of our present predicament, he said without hesitation that we would have to go to Casablanca and there catch an overwater flight around Spain to England.

Having told me that, he went over to the operations board, studied it a minute, made some changes in the figures, and then picked up a phone. I heard him tell someone to unload eight hundred pounds of freight from a certain flight, and then he hung up and rejoined me. He explained apologetically that he would have to have the

names and serial numbers of all four of us—"Bloody
regulations, you know"—and that it would be an hour and
a half before takeoff time. Would that be all right, Johnny?
Just like that! With no fuss or hooraw, this Englishman,
who knew me only casually and whom I hadn't seen for
nearly a year, gave the system a whack and got me and my
buddies on our way.

We were in Casablanca by midmorning the next day, and
we learned that we could get new bookings on an ATC
flight out for England in two or three days. This was a
major terminal, and we were asked no questions as to how
we came to be there. Since we were authorized to fly, there
was no problem with scheduling.

Exotic, romantic Casablanca! I guess there wasn't a man
in all of 67th Group who hadn't seen the Ingrid Bergman-
Humphrey Bogart movie *Casablanca* at least three times in
our year and a half in England. The name of the place had
the kind of romantic magic to it that stirs the innocent
mind, like Paris and Budapest and Istanbul. And here we
were with time on our hands!

So right after breakfast the next morning the four of us
hired an open horse-drawn cab for a sight-seeing tour of the
town. It was a tired-looking rig but with just the right touch
of faded elegance about it. We hadn't gone four blocks,
though, before my allergy to horses set me to sneezing, so
with eyes watering I got out and sent the rest of the guys
on their way. I went into a nearby salon-bar to have a drink
while I waited out my allergy seizure.

The place was dim to my eyes after the harsh morning
sunlight outside, but I could make out the high ceiling with
three old-fashioned fans languidly stirring the stale air; the
whitewashed walls and ceiling, cracked and gray; and a
long bar, suitably scarred and time-worn, that ran along the
left wall. The bartender wore a soiled fez, as did several of
the blank-faced men grouped at two tables, drinks before
them, smoke coiling up from their long, thin cigars.

As I took this all in I could imagine that the piano
tinkling somewhere in the back of the room had just finished playing "As Time Goes By," and I suppressed an

impulse to call out, "Play it again, Sam!" But my eyes had adjusted to the inside light, and I saw that it was a player piano clinking aimlessly on. I also noticed that the flies greatly outnumbered the customers, and when one plunked into the glass of wine I'd been served, I walked out of the place.

I wandered down a side street, keeping in the shade, determined to find some of the true romantic flavor I knew must be there, and the sight of a woman across the street brought me up short. She wore a white burnous, the flowing, graceful, ankle-length robe that drapes over the head and across the lower half of the face, a truly exotic and quite beautiful garment. This woman carried on her head a tall jar, which her left hand steadied as she walked along with a fluid grace, her right arm swinging to the rhythm of her gait. Though she was too far away for me to see her few exposed facial features, I imagined black eyes sparkling under modestly lowered long lashes. Ah, the enchanting beauty, the seductress of the Casbah: There it was, all the mystery of Casablanca embodied in this graceful woman. And as I watched with growing excitement, she abruptly stopped and scratched her ass vigorously with her right hand.

So much for exotic, romantic, flea-bitten Casablanca; Bogart could have it. By now the heat was oppressive, and the flies, busily investigating the open sores on the hordes of half-naked children playing in the street and then reporting to me, were intolerable, so I took a taxi back to the air base. I spent the rest of my time in Casablanca alternately pestering the flight dispatcher, drinking warm Cokes, and eating cardboard doughnuts at the Red Cross canteen.

On the evening of our second full day there, we were alerted, and were off the next morning in a B-24 converted for passenger service. This flight was to take us to Newquay, a field named after a resort town located near Penzance in Cornwall in the extreme southwest part of England. This route was used because the flight had to circle out around the Iberian Peninsula to avoid neutral Spain and Portugal and the deadly JU-88 hunter-killers the Germans sent out over the Bay of Biscay from France. This made Newquay the closest safe English point available to the Casablanca flight.

Late in the afternoon I woke from a nap and looked out of my porthole to see a sight I shall be a long time forgetting. We had turned somewhat to the west, and there, not many miles away through the channel mist, I saw that magnificent cool green that is England's own, the greenest green in the world. It was so beautiful, so welcoming, and so charged with personal significance that I felt tears smarting at my eyes.

36

We stepped out of the plane onto a ramp swept by a gusty wind bearing the promise of September fog and rain. The wind cut through my light khakis, but I savored the damp feel of it. England! I wanted to jump into the air, to kiss the ground, to shout for joy. The two previous winters I had cursed that supersaturated bone-chilling stuff that passes for air in England, but just then I thought I had never felt anything so sweet.

We were driven immediately to a small resort hotel that served as transient quarters and were told that we would be given orders, instructions, and plane accommodations to London the next morning. The first person I thought to phone was Dick Frost, an RAF intelligence officer I knew at Middle Wallop's RAF sector control. By good luck I got him at once, and he told me that the 107th Squadron had moved to the continent shortly after D day. He didn't know where they were now, but I must come down to Middle Wallop the first chance I got, and I promised I would.

At dinner I learned that there was a dance scheduled that evening, some sort of joint Anglo-American officers' lash-up, at one of the hotels nearby. I wasn't invited, but the coincidence of a special party on the day of my return to England seemed a good omen, so I decided to go. That I was dressed in secondhand-issue khakis in this land where wool-

ens were uniform the year around, had not even a necktie
to lend a suggestion of formality, and was still wearing .
those black RAF boots with steel heelplates, bothered me
not a bit. I was wearing the only clothes I had; there was a
party shaping up; I went.

It was, as any self-respecting, down-home Hoosier would
put it, a right elegant party, with an orchestra, women in
formals, and a bar. About an equal number of RAF and
American officers were there, some pilots among them;
and rank ran all the way from lieutenant to colonel. Newquay
had been, at one time, a resort town of some prominence,
and this hotel was quite posh, or so it seemed to me at the
time. I immediately worked my way to the bar, and on the
way I saw disapproval in the faces of the Americans who
noticed me. Englishmen, of course, simply do not register
any reaction to the bizarre.

At the bar I found myself next to an RAF group captain,
a pilot wearing the British Distinguished Flying Cross. He
made room for me and was friendly enough in the way he
passed the time of day with me, but I had the feeling that
although he was not actually inviting me to explain myself,
he would be interested in knowing just what the hell I
meant by crashing a formal party in that garb.

By that time I was self-conscious beside all the class A
uniforms with their brass gleaming in the soft light. So after
I got my drink, I explained to the group captain what my
situation was and why I had joined the party. I admitted
that I must have looked pretty grotesque, and suggested
lamely that I would just have a drink and leave.

Englishmen have an unusual capacity for rising to an
occasion, and this officer came through true to form, generously and magnificently. He not only refused to hear of my
leaving, he instructed the bartender to refuse my money
and charge all my drinks to him. He went further, introduc-
ing me to other RAF people there, making it clear that I
was his guest. He must have passed the word about my
circumstances to Americans and British alike, because things
grew progressively friendlier as the evening wore on.

The homecoming celebration was a great success, and as

we droned through the next day's lovely drizzle towar
London, my heart was gay. London was the most excitin
place I had ever seen. I liked its somber, enduring arrogance
its surprising patterns, its orderliness even in the extreme
of war, and its courteous policemen. There was somethin
especially reassuring about the unbelievable din of Hyd
Park's antiaircraft batteries when the big guns went t
work at night on a German air attack. So I was perfectl
happy to be headed there for the cleansing ritual that woul
get my name and status straightened out in the militar
files, after which the administrative machinery would plo
through the process that would yield orders disposing o
me one way or another.

On my first free day, now fully uniformed, outfitted, an
paid, I hustled out to Paddington Station and got a train t
Andover, and from there I took a cab to Middle Wallop
The field had been taken over by the RAF, and it was no
difficult to locate Frost and settle down for a long talk.

Dick Frost and I had become friends shortly after ou
group moved to Middle Wallop and went into comba
operations. On our first acquaintance, he introduced me t
the wondrous workings of RAF fighter control, the bes
coordinating machine of its kind in the world at that time
Dick had shown me everything in the area there was to see
including the historic treasures guarded in a cottage som
miles away by one Mr. Lawrence Tanner, "Keeper of th
Muniments of Westminster Abbey." Among those price
less relics, taken away from the abbey to avoid possibl
destruction by bombing, was an indenture signed by Rich
ard III, and Dick had me place my hand at the spot dread
ful King Richard had placed his to sign the document.

Dick brought me up to date on the fortunes of the war
and of his family. Little Budgie, his laughing tot of a daugh
ter who had showed me how to gather wildflowers, wa
well and had prayed for me. We talked and drank tea lat
into the night.

I went back to London the next morning and spent th
rest of the day going from office to office trying to get a lin
on my squadron, with no luck. Nobody knew where it wa

and no one cared. Hell, it was just another combat outfit. I did arrange for five days' leave, certain that somehow I could locate and get to the squadron.

That evening at the Red Cross Jules Club I ran into Bob Mulligan, adjutant of my former squadron, and we decided to eat in high style, at Odennino's. We finished late, and just toward the end of the meal the sirens cranked up. "Air raid warning red" was announced diffidently, but no one paid any attention. At this late date in the game Jerry sent in only an occasional tip-and-run attack on the city, as if to let England know he was still a contestant. An ME-109 carrying one bomb would come pissing in from a great height over the channel, drop his load willy-nilly, and bug out, if he was lucky.

Bob and I had just got out into the foyer when the Hyde Park batteries, just a few blocks away, opened up. They made a horrendous racket, sending up tons of explosives, which all returned to earth in a tinkling hail of steel scrap. We could hear this tintinnabulating shower under the thunder of the guns, and we knew we would have to wait inside until the row was over and all that had gone up had come down.

The foyer soon filled up with other diners waiting for the letup, and I noticed particularly a young Englishman with his girl standing near us. They were a good-looking couple, but the man was becoming more impatient by the minute. I saw him shoot his cuff to look at his watch for the nth time and heard him growl to the girl, "Oh, blast the bloody Hun! Now we shall be late!"

37

The next morning I started my rounds again and was luck
right at the start. In the Piccadilly subway station I ran int
a pilot I knew from 67th Group operations, and he told m
that the 107th was on airstrip 46 just outside Versailles
near Paris. He also told me about a courier plane that flew
from Herndon to A-46 and other points along the way. Thi
courier occasionally carried passengers, he thought. I heade
for Herndon, just on the edge of London, without anothe
thought.

In the operations office of the courier outfit, I found tha
the man I had to deal with was an Air Corps ground office
who wore, along with his European theater ribbon, a good
conduct ribbon and a sharpshooter's medal. Hell! I thought
I'm in for trouble! I was right.

The captain listened to my story with a look of studie
interest on his face, but gazed out the window all the while
his right profile to me, elbows resting on the chair arms an
his fingertips steepled in front of his face. When I wa
through, he thought for a moment, then began the kind o
talk I'd had too many times before from principals an
deans, the this-hurts-me-more-than-it-hurts-you routine, s
as soon as I could, I made for the door and closed it behin
me. Never get into a pissing contest with a skunk, I'
heard my grandad say.

I went over to the sergeant who was making like busy at a desk and asked, "Where the hell did you find him?" jerking my thumb in the direction of the captain's closed door.

He looked up, embarrassed, then down at his own good-conduct ribbon and said, "He makes me wear it. He ain't real bad, though. When I have to walk in the street with him I just make like I don't know him, and I slip the ribbon off the clip, like this, see? Like I lost it. Look, Lieutenant," he said in a lower voice and quickly, "go to hangar 8 and ask for Lieutenant Goodwin and tell him what you need," and he went back to rustling papers.

I found hangar 8 and Lieutenant Goodwin easily enough, and when I told him about my encounter with the captain, he just looked at me. I'm sure he realized he couldn't think of anything to say that hadn't already occurred to me. Finally he said, "Be here at three sharp. This is the bucket that stops at A-46," and gestured to a C-47 nearby.

A little while after takeoff we were over the unbelievable jumble of Omaha Beach, and I couldn't believe that the torn-up countryside just beyond was the same peaceful-looking bit of France I had flown over often just five months ago. I knew that real estate well; I was one of the small group of fliers who had photographed the area in strips to make the so-called Merton grids used for artillery fire control during the initial invasion stages.

The whole trip was an eye-popping revelation. I hadn't thought it possible the Allies could get as much stuff ashore as I saw down there. And at every airstrip there was a long train of C-47 transport planes in the pattern to land, three and four at a time on final approach.

It was early evening when the plane landed at A-46 and taxied over to the squadron area. A score of tents were there, and a few bomb-wrecked buildings, and it all looked drab and unfamiliar except for the trim, long-nosed P-51s scattered along the hardstanding. Well, I thought as I looked over the layout, this is the end of the line, the place I have been breaking my neck to get back to since the third of

May. Four months and six days later I'm back where I belong!

As I walked toward the tents, I was afraid that no one here would know me. Maybe all the old bunch had been rotated home or killed, and I'd find only replacements who would stare with polite curiosity at my questions. As these uneasy thoughts were going through my mind, a familiar figure came gangling up the tent row with the duty-officer brassard on his arm, followed by one of the enlisted men.

"MacTarvish!" I yelled. It was MacAllister, formerly my flight commander. He came up to me and, in the zany way he had, put his arms akimbo and glowered at me from under his helmet.

"Hickman, goddamit! We got word day before yesterday that you were dead. What are you trying to do, fuck up the paperwork?" Then he broke into a big smile, stuck out his hand, and said, "Johnny boy, it's good to see you! By God, we knew you'd make it! But what the hell took you so long? Come on in—to hell with the mail, Sergeant, just burn it—come on, Johnny. The other guys are all at the movie down in the cellar, but they'll be out in a little bit. We can open up a jar in the meantime. How the hell are you?"

Mac led me into one of the partially wrecked buildings, holding my arm and talking the whole time. Frank Dillon was on R and R in the States, as were Dick Booze and Jack Chapin and Joe Hulday. John Hoefker was on rest leave in England, and no longer with the 107th. Rod Patton and Turner had been shot down and were known to be prisoners, and Mac named off six of the old crowd who had been killed. Losses had been heavy, and just that day my former crew chief had lost his third plane. He was feeling pretty low; would I go have a talk with him?

The rangy Texan talked on and on, occasionally interrupting his recital of squadron news to pound me on the back and exclaim, "Goddamit, Hickman, we knew you would make it!" Finally the scraping of chairs in the room downstairs announced the end of the movie, and soon the fellows began to drift into the club room. I looked eagerly at their faces, most of them looking tired as they came through the door, but the first few arrivals were strangers.

And suddenly there was Dick Kile, who had flown wing with me on my last mission. Dick saw me as soon as he came through the door, and he stopped dead for a second, an expression of worry clouding his face. Abruptly he moved toward me saying, as though he were talking about something that had happened only yesterday, "Hickman, I want to tell you what happened—" As he talked rapidly on, his face serious, it dawned on me that he believed that somehow he had been responsible for my being shot down. I took pains to explain that it was my own damn foolishness, and no fault of his, that had brought on my trouble.

As others came in and the drinks began to circulate, the feeling of being in a strange place faded and then disappeared completely. Snort Atkins, the squadron CO, was there, and Cook with his crazy jokes, and No-No Anderson, the intelligence officer who had assured me that my last mission would be a milk run. There were other pilots I knew, raw replacements when I had last seen them, but now veterans of fifty and sixty missions. It was deeply satisfying to sit with those fellows and hear the familiar talk, talk spiced with the private jokes and cliches that a group of men will develop out of their individual personalities and make a part of the group personality. No mistaking it, this was the 107th! During this session I learned that I had been awarded the Distinguished Flying Cross. Anderson went to his office and brought back a copy of the orders with the comment that he had held them instead of sending them to my home because he knew I would be back.

It was the end of a long road, and I was tired and very much in need of rest. But I was back! And these were my old buddies! And this was France! So after a few hours in the club, I piled onto Kile's motorcycle with him and we roared off into the night to Paris.

EPILOGUE

My request to be taken back into the 107th Squadron for continued combat duty was refused. The 67th Group commander explained to me that my having been a prisoner of the Germans put me in jeopardy should they again capture me, since the Geneva Convention allowed them to shoot me as a spy under those circumstances.

So I caught the courier plane back to London, and within a week I was on a ship for New York. I was allowed a couple weeks at home in Indiana with my wife and parents and brother Bob, in his senior year at high school and impatient to get into the war himself.

Mary Lee and I drove down to the Air Corps redistribution center in Miami Beach for another cleansing ritual—physical exams, interrogation, and psychological testing (had the war unhinged me?)—and an onward assignment as an instructor at Luke Field, an advanced flight training base near Phoenix, Arizona. After less than three months there, I was transferred to Key Field, near Meridian, Mississippi, with an operational training unit flying Mustangs.

Shortly after V-J day (August 15, 1945), while I was still at Key Field, a large file of bills I'd signed for in Switzerland arrived through military channels. They'd found me after all! So after a bit of quibbling I slapped my money order on the heap and back it went to Switzerland, and my last open account with the war was closed.

In early November my wife and I drove up to Baer Field, near Fort Wayne, Indiana, not fifteen miles from my parents' home, for my processing out of the service. I was put on terminal leave beginning November 10, and made an inactive reservist effective December 10. I was a civilian again! —four years, ten months, and ten days after that first bunch of us had been sent off from Columbia City with a town chorus singing, "Good-bye, dear, I'll be back in a year."